# Everlasting

## "Love" – That is

> *Jack: ...*"We Have the Highest & Deepest Love
>
> *That Two Souls Can Bathe In"*
>
> ...God's Love

*"Divine Love"*

## The Continuation of Love From the Other Side

## Part III

By Dorothy and Jack Farley

Balboa Press books may be ordered through booksellers or by contacting:

Balboa Press
A Division of Hay House
1663 Liberty Drive
Bloomington, IN 47403
www.balboapress.com
1 (877) 407-4847

Because of the dynamic nature of the Internet, any web addresses or links contained in this book may have changed since publication and may no longer be valid. The views expressed in this work are solely those of the author and do not necessarily reflect the views of the publisher, and the publisher hereby disclaims any responsibility for them.

The author of this book does not dispense medical advice or prescribe the use of any technique as a form of treatment for physical, emotional, or medical problems without the advice of a physician, either directly or indirectly. The intent of the author is only to offer information of a general nature to help you in your quest for emotional and spiritual well-being. In the event you use any of the information in this book for yourself, which is your constitutional right, the author and the publisher assume no responsibility for your actions.

Any people depicted in stock imagery provided by Thinkstock are models, and such images are being used for illustrative purposes only. Certain stock imagery © Thinkstock.

Printed in the United States of America.

ISBN: 978-1-4525-1446-8 (sc)
ISBN: 978-1-4525-1448-2 (hc)
ISBN: 978-1-4525-1447-5 (e)

Library of Congress Control Number: 2014908896

Balboa Press rev. date: 06/03/2014

## Our Extraordinary Life

Nothing about our Life is
"Ordinary". Our rewards are also
"Extraordinary".

Our Life is
saturated with meaning and purpose.
There could be no Better Life.

*Dorothy and
Jack*

ALL PROCEEDS FROM THE SALE OF THIS BOOK GO TO **CAT HAVEN** CHARITABLE TRUST, RESORT FOR CATS & WILDLIFE PRESERVE - OUR MISSION AND PASSION TO MAKE THIS WORLD A BETTER PLACE. OUR LOVE FOR THE ANIMAL KINGDOM WILL REMAIN OUR BLISS FOR ETERNITY.

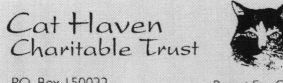

Cat Haven
Charitable Trust

P.O. Box 150022
Austin, Texas 78715

Resort For Cats
& Wildlife Preserve

# "Everlasting, Love—That Is"
## — The Continuation of Love From the Other Side — Part III

Cover Illustration is a channeled healing energy by Dorothy and Jack Farley for Dorothy, done October 5, 2010. Dorothy had asked Spirit that this healing energy be for herself. (In their first book, Listen, I'm Still Here – Part I, in which Jack began his appearance in butterfly form and allowed Dorothy to kiss his wings – for her, the butterfly is symbolic.)

## ACKNOWLEDGEMENTS AND BIBLIOGRAPHY

We are pleased to acknowledge permission to reprint a brief quotation from the following works:

The Lockman Foundation. Copyright 1983. New American

# PREFACE

"There's a great deal of beauty in the loving, giving, responsible kind of person you are likely to be now or are working to become. Others usually recognize and appreciate your feeling nature and your desire and ability to aid and comfort others. As you get older, you may learn to combine the beauty of the responsible side of your personality with the special sensitivity of the intuitive, spiritually aware part of your character. As you learn, you're apt to find much satisfaction in your life. As you mature, you'll probably give much to other people and, if you choose, also develop your special spiritual gifts."

*This is a numerology report summary, 2012-2013 for Dorothy Farley*
Paul Minar, Numerologist, Teacher, Author
"Numbers, The Energy Forces in Your Name" (iuniverse.com)
Email: personalnumbers@gmail.com
Website: www.numbersbypaulminar.com
(530) 820-3129

§

"You are the embodiment of love. That is what you teach."
Shakti Miller, ND, LCSW
Lifeforce Healing & Counseling
shaktimiller@gmail.com
www.shaktimiller.com
(512) 328-0814

§

*Remember, I am with you always until the end of time.*
*— Matthew 28:20*

# FOREWARD

**APRIL 7, 2013**
**Jack's words to me**
*Jack: We have the highest and deepest love that two souls can bathe in…*

When my husband told me this (I had written it in haste on a scrap of paper); I <u>knew instantly</u> that there was a third book yet to be written by us.

On this particular day when this message was received, I had been expressing out loud, as I do every day, my appreciation and gratitude for Jack's goodness to me – he had done and given so much that was 'visible' – <u>for the customers of our company</u> (Heart Construction) through his building and creations for them – <u>on our land</u> in the creation of our sanctuary – <u>his Vietnam War heroism for his country</u> – and the 'invisible' held securely in my heart and soul. Jack was a giving man, a pure man, a cool and calm man. His values were always so in line with biblical teaching and although I had heard and read much for myself, these teachings were embedded in him and could not be denied. It was always comforting to be near him when I was troubled by anything – and I mean anything. His understanding was deep, his acceptance profound; he always had the perfect answer on the tip of his tongue and his glistening eyes revealed <u>his knowing</u> of their truth. His slightest touch washed your cares away.

I am so blessed that he is my eternal soulmate, and he continues to surprise me and maintain my attention and learning. With this particular statement, "***highest and deepest***," he is speaking of God's love – and yes we all have it. That perfect Divine love, undying, never-ending, Everlasting "Love" – that is, when we allow, and accept it.

I remain immersed in this new found level of 'bathing' whenever I repeat his words to myself, and yes I am seeing clearly that <u>others have doubt about this wonderment</u> – <u>OF GOD'S LOVE, in which I choose to live</u>.

<u>We must all learn to live in that fearless space.</u> <u>It is there for</u>

us, ALL OF US – not just me. It is our doubting that holds us back. I have days when I forget and have to reconnect, for I am still in the flesh. Reconnection is simple, swift, blink of an eye, instantly freeing from the ties that we allow to bind us. "I'm sorry God," I say, and the connection is remade and all is well again. Living in God's power & resting 'without doubt' in His love, is the only space in which to be.

We all have free will and must learn to make right choices. Once again, this level of living in God's love – it is simply a matter of choice. God's love is for everyone, everywhere. God bless your choices.

§

**I am going to finish everything God has called me to do. Therefore, we are now starting Part III of my conversations with my beloved Jack.**

This, our third book, would appear to be the beginning of the end of our words of expression – in printed form – that is for Dorothy and Jack Farley, regarding the growth of our souls.

God has us in the palm of His hand and the *"highest and deepest love that two souls can bathe in"* has our bathing at an entirely different level of understanding.

For me, Dorothy Farley, while still in the flesh, I am in overwhelm with satisfaction whenever I allow this level of understanding to fulfill my being. I am told by my beloved Jack, while he is in Spirit, that the best is still yet to come. He would always say this when he was with me on Earth, but I believe that when I join him in Heaven – I will be able to fly much higher than I am. The completion of purpose, the soul's perfection, is beyond imagination, but I am open to receiving the fulfillment knowing I have done God's Will.

**It is our sincere hope that your choice to read our words will bring you comfort, tears of joy, laughter and learning.**

§

GRATITUDE TO:

- GOD, and His abundant grace
- JACK – my beloved who is always 'Here', while being 'There'
- ANIMALS – and lessons learned from them – for the growth of my soul
- NATURE – Others have said, and I agree, there must be places for animals and human beings to satisfy their souls (CAT HAVEN is a place and space for a few of God's creatures to enjoy peace and know love)
- ME – Where my love of the Animal Kingdom surpasses most human understanding. I love them "completely".

*Jack: It is only those in high places of understanding who work with the animals. You are in a high place of understanding. You are blessed Sweetheart, your work is blessed and so are you. Few hearts can give to the lowest hearts of understanding.*

**- Page 121,** *I'm Always Here,* **Part II**
Continuation of Love from the Other Side

# DEDICATION

**TO <u>GOD</u>**
and His Will for our life

§

**'MY' JACK**
his teachings while on earth
and now from Heaven

§

**WORLD-WIDE CONSERVATION
PRESERVATION
PROTECTION & RESCUE**

§

For us (Jack and I), it is preservation and protection of God's creation
– the animal kingdom – on our small parcel of land.

**All creatures great and small, our Lord God made them all.**

It is Jack's and my way of making this world a safer
and better place for all creatures who come here.

Our reward is knowing we are doing GOD'S WILL.

We learn from these creatures and see that they learn from us,
by the love reflected in their eyes.

§

# ILLUMINATION

*"Dying is progression to a higher level.*
*The possessiveness of life, selfishness, jealousy, resentment*
*– these have been dropped with the old garment of the body.*
*Spirit now has new work to do.  So have we – to make*
*the most of the rest of our lives until we join you."*

*- Author Unknown*

# INTRODUCTION

Here it is now six years after the transition of my beloved husband and soulmate. I was becoming aware that I was changing, certainly in my understanding. Since God had me in the palm of His hand, my learning was deep, acute and transforming. Life and its meaning was beginning to reveal that meaning to me and not necessarily to others around me, for they did not have the pain or had not cried the tears that I had, and they did not see as my eyes were seeing. There was a definite disconnect from me to others.

This continued growth is detailed in our first two books – *Listen, I'm Still*, Part I and *I'm Always Here*, Part II wherein I had become aware, through my Jack, of the continuation of love, life, living and learning with our loved ones on the other side. We are eternal spirit beings, and this is possible when we choose to live as God desires for us – <u>a life without fear and consumed only by His Love</u>.

The publishing company had requested I write an article about this loss – the loss of a soulmate or a loved one, and if one could ever get over it. The following is my truth:

2012
**To the World I Say**

<u>**MY TRUTH**</u>:
**NO! NOT REALLY, AND CERTAINLY 'NOT COMPLETELY'!**

<u>HOWEVER</u>, with the passing of time (for me, now six years) one's understanding deepens, and the gradual 'acceptance' that we are all spirit beings with eternal life awakens within us, and *"everything is as it should be"*. There is no ending at death.

At the time of 'their' transition, <u>our thought process</u> – of necessity – changes. <u>We</u> begin to see things differently, and this expansion brings an intermittent level of peace. We lose friends who are not aware of this necessary change in our understanding – which is needed for our continued existence here on the Earth realm.

Real growth and the reason for our being here on this Earth begins to shine forth for us and reveal life's profound meaning, and <u>why we are here</u>. We see more clearly the only two emotions, '**FEAR**' or '**LOVE**'. We begin the process of releasing negatives – the fears hidden within us since our childhood that have held back our growth. Our eyes open, and we see mistakes – previous misunderstandings. We extend forgiveness to others. We ask forgiveness for ourselves, and, we 'accept' forgiveness, and then the heart can open to a new level of **LOVE**. Our vibration changes – some days we can fly. We begin opening our heart to more **LOVE** – **LOVE** for everything around us, **LOVE** for everyone we meet, for everything we see and do, and for ourselves. <u>Let's not forget ourselves.</u> We remember "***<u>LOVE is all there is</u>***".

Staying in the **LOVE VIBRATION** is what I have learned to do, and this is where I can reach and connect with the responsive vibration of my beloved husband. He assures me, "***We are never apart, <u>only in our minds</u>***." This is the same for all people. Anyone can make this connection – it is a matter of choice – <u>our choice</u>, for our loved ones are always here around us in many forms; it is up to us to open our heart to the deepest, <u>most pure **LOVE**,</u> and in so doing elevate our vibration to reaching and hearing them. This is possible, <u>if we</u> make the choice.

Taking time to "***listen***" to their response does take quality attentiveness, and we must be in a fearless and worry-free space. <u>They hear us ALWAYS</u>, but we do not hear them. I have learned to stay in the space of grace and gratitude where healing of mind and body can take place. I choose to live in the good memories knowing that when <u>we</u> have memory recall, so too do our loved ones. "***Every memory we had with them is embedded in their soul.***"

We cry for ourselves! The pain – we allow ourselves to feel – is for 'us', not our departed loved ones. We know their new space (dimension, realm, level of understanding) is without pain. We pour forth our grief at OUR LOSS of 'THEIR GOODNESS'. We have regrets; they have none. For when it is 'their time' to move on ahead of us, they are ready! 'Their best', this time around in this incarnation (lifetime), has been accomplished – it is complete. We need to thank God for our 'coming together' with 'them' in this lifetime, and know 'they' will be the first to greet us when it is our time to join them 'on the other side'. For now, remember – *"We are ONE with the LOVE and the joy of God. Remember only this joy, and there I will be with you. I am always with you."*

P.S. Even when these TRUTHS are known and understood, it is all easier said than done but becomes more permanently possible as time goes by, and the light of a new future shines forth. This is the time when we make our departed loved ones happy!

§

THIS, OUR THIRD BOOK,
WILL HOPEFULLY RELAY THAT
LOVE **IS** EVERLASTING
AND ALL THAT THERE REALLY IS.
GOD IS LOVE, AND WE ARE **ONE WITH GOD**.
YES, OPEN YOUR EYES TO THIS LEVEL OF UNDERSTANDING.
TAKE IT AND FLY.
TAKE TIME TO PERFECT YOUR SOUL,
NOT YOUR BODY – FOR THAT IS NOT WHO YOU ARE.

§

*This is what I write with hardly any light in the middle of the night.*

# TABLE OF CONTENTS

**2012 - 2014**

**FEBRUARY 2013**

· 'Thank You's' galore
· My new space for being
· My elegant life
· I am glad I hear Jack's promptings
· *Ching* is an absolute angel
· It could not be better

**MARCH 2013**

· Hummingbirds are coming
· Rewards for our work
· My faith account is full
· I know who is in charge
· I'm not happy when our babies don't come home to me
· Still no *Gus* or *Linen*
· *Linen* is back home at **CAT HAVEN**
· My personal growth
· The sweetness of you is missed beyond words

**APRIL 2013**

· Where I live
· I see the reflection of me through the cats
· Finally, we have printer proofs of our second book, *I'm Always Here*
· Today you touched me, and I knew it
· Our first radio interview and I loved it
· Once again, I am in 'your chair'. I love it here.
· I'm hurting myself to please God, and I know that is not right

**MAY 20**

· Our beloved *China* went to heaven today
· To the World I Say
· It may be *Happy's* time to come home
· *Happy's* timing
· *Happy* is on his way to heaven today

**JUNE 2013**

· My husband was never late for anything!
· More miracles from *Mittens*
· Thank you God for the priviledge of our beloved *Harpo*
· Rich rewards – our *Rozie-Bear* knows he is loved
· Wow, stupid me
· How incredible is nature

# CHAPTER 1
## 2012

# I HAVE LITTLE MEMORY OF
# WHAT I WRITE

5<sup>th</sup> year of conversation after Jack's transition

# ILLUMINATION

*Let us insist on raising funds*

*of LOVE,*

*of KINDNESS,*

*of UNDERSTANDING,*

*of PEACE.*

*Money will come*

*if we SEEK FIRST*

*the KINGDOM OF GOD.*

*— Mother Teresa*

**JUNE 14, 2012 – 10:35 P.M.**
**Wonders never cease – for me!**

Me (to Jack): I want to know how you feel about what happened today – our second book is finished and some self-published books are being printed this date. Not too many because last time (with Part I) I went overboard and still have copies of *Listen, I'm Still Here* on hand! I feel confident I will sell (or give) them down the road. I truly do not worry about that.

*Jack: Good girl, my girl, my remarkable girl, lady and wife. Like you, I am somewhat in a state of disbelief at your accomplishment.*

Me: OUR accomplishment. I have had to proof this book several times of late, and I have very little recollection of what we said. I can remember many of my questions, but your answers are literally out of this world with love and wisdom. You always were smart, but you excel now. Wow, wowee is what I write on just about every page. This, our second book, has 541 pages – which is a huge book and can be intimidating to a lot of people – I'm sure; and, of course, the price will be high, but honestly Sweetheart, I don't care about that. I did, we did, what God asked us to do. We used our creative talent, and He said He would give us everything needed. I did my part, you did yours, and we did ours together – now it is up to God. It is so much more expensive to get a book published than I ever imagined, but I will allow God to take it where He wants it. My worries have to be over. I am just now, this very day – with Michele's quality help, putting together the marketing plan for *Listen, I'm Still Here* – Part I. I am going to make myself available to promote this come August 20, 2012 for three or four months. I'm not quite sure. I cannot travel, and I don't want to travel because of the animals, so we shall see what they can do! It is up to God now – truly. I am giving a copy of this book (Sweetheart, it is a work of art in design, layout and the wisdom – I am so, so proud) to Mr. Richard Fuller, the publicist from last year who gave us a 5-star rating for *Listen, I'm Still Here* – Part I. I am hoping on that for Part II. I believe the same publisher will publish for us.

*Jack: Oh they will, don't doubt it.*

Me: It is a big book, and the sales may be limited.

*Jack: Don't think that way Baby, don't go there. The presentation is beyond perfect and impressive. The right people are there ready to receive it.*

Me: Tomorrow, Michele will bring me six copies of the self-published book, bound as a book is bound, and 10 copies with plastic binding. The cover, front and back, are just plain beautiful. One of our cruise pictures, do you remember with the moonlight in the background, is on the back cover.

*Jack: Yes I do. It was one you wanted so badly.*

Me: I am wearing that white crochet dress you became tired of, and you look strikingly handsome in evening attire. The quotation from God that accompanies it is as follows:

*I had said to God one day as I was walking down the driveway:*

> Me: "God, I miss my husband so much. He was perfect for me. He may not have been perfect for anyone else, but he was perfect for me."
> **GOD: "He still is perfect for you, My Child, perfect for what I want you to do. You are a perfect couple united for My Work."**

*Jack: <u>My goodness, that is something special, isn't it?</u>*

Me: It sure is, and our book and those words with photos of real butterflies taken from the jar I have right next to our bed, are also on the cover. Butterflies represent how <u>you</u> reveal your presence to me so often.

*Jack: I did not know this. <u>I am with you all the time, and how I appear to you was unknown to me until this moment</u>. I am glad I please you because you certainly please me.*

§

## JUNE 16, 2012

Me: I want a gentleman friend now who has interest in being the best he can be. I want a man who has interest in what Jack has to tell me.
**GOD: He is there My Child, he is there.**

§

# CHAPTER 2
# 2012

# I REMEMBER HIS CHAIR
**5th year of conversation after Jack's transition**

# ILLUMINATION

*Discover the Will of God*

*for your life,*

*and walk in it.*

**JUNE 16, 2012 – 10:15 A.M.**
**I remember 'his chair'**

Me:  Long hours of sitting in 'his chair'
Anxious most nights to finish chores so that I could get to sit in 'his chair'.

I remember peace while being there in 'his chair'.

I remember mornings seeing my notebook on the seat of 'his chair' which meant I had been up during the night writing, because when I write at night I always put my notebook to the side on his table.

I remember good sleep after being in 'his chair', with him – a satisfaction that my heart knew of – but when reading my notes the following day, I had little memory of the conversation. It was all 'new' to me too. And now, seeing the book, *I'm Always Here*, in its final form it is like, "WHO WROTE THIS?"

I am just God's instrument, but I do choose to listen.
It is possible for all to hear if they make that choice.
It is a choice that any can make.

§

7

## JUNE 21, 2012
## The beauty of it is

Me:  Today it is my birthday, and I am 77 years young.

Today I buried two of my most precious babies.

Dear Sweet *Tuff-Tuffin* was found early this morning before 8:30 A.M. leaning over the deer waterpans at *Trough I*. It is my choice of belief that he went to the waterpans to get a drink and had some sort of stroke. He was leaning on the pan and the table and I believe was so vulnerable, that a night creature came and harmed his back leg. I don't believe he was harmed before he fell. To my hands, he felt warm and still pliable.

The beauty of it is that just last night, I personally handed him more than one plate of canned foods to select from, and I personally placed before him his favorite dry food. He ate well and did not seem to be in any discomfort other than the heat. The night before, he was sleeping on a high roof of one of the buildings. Yesterday his friends were around him all day. He was on the driveway to greet me in the early morning. The beauty of it is he lived to the last moment. This allows me to feel peace. (He and his sister *Muff-Muffin* were found under a vehicle at an automotive shop near to the vets' office in the mid-nineties. In human years, Tuff was in his 90s. He had been with me since he was a kitten.)

Darling *Mackie*, my last orange Tabby, was not well this day at all. To me, he has been the strongest, smallest cat I have had. *Mackie* loves to eat and has done so very well until this past week. Just last night I tempted him with at least five favorites including two different baby foods – and the same this morning. He did eat two or three tuna crunchies today, and that was his last food. Both times when I was with him he did enjoy the petting.

It was my decision to ask the services of the Trust Veterinarian, Dr. Ron Stried, and he took time from his schedule this afternoon to come to the property and put our darling *Mackie* to sleep. It went very smoothly and I felt peace within myself at my decision. *Mackie* was hurting today; all he wanted was loving, and I gave as much as I was able to; he has many brothers and sisters, but today I gave 'him' extra.

The beauty of it is that just within the past month, the last month of dear *Mackie's* life, he had at his age caught two huge birds and I witnessed him strutting around showing his 'catch' to his friends. I allowed this for Jack had told me years ago that when a bird is caught by a cat, it usually means the bird is weak in some way. Our beautiful *Mackie* was so strong to the end of his life – running the length of the driveway to our house every day to see me (and receive baby food). And like *Tuff*, he had a very good life.

My beloved Jack was here today in butterfly form outside one of the buildings. I know he was here to wish me a happy birthday. And the beauty of it is, these two cats are now at peace and without pain.

Let it be known I have had two cats transition in a week before, but never two in a day. It is not easy work God has me doing, but my heart is full - chocablock full of wonderful memories. Jack, take over. *Jack: Baby, my wonderful wife and best friend, what a good job you did today. You have never been so strong yourself and yes I was there all day, but thought it just right to reveal my presence when you were heading toward the Ruffhouse. Little Frenly is a 'big boy' that is for sure* (I was putting *Frenly*, one of our newest and youngest babies, into his house). *He loves you Baby, they all do, and especially me!*

§

**LATER**

Me: Everything, absolutely everything I had never had, I had with you Jack – true love, pure love, unselfish love – GOD'S LOVE.
*Jack: Me too Baby, me too.*
Me: The more you refine yourself, the more refined you become. I endeavor to refine for spiritual reasons, not just a healthy body.

§

**JUNE 22, 2012**
**This is how I think**

Me: **The greatest gift we can receive or give – as I see it**:
But what have we done to be ready to receive our Divine inheritance? We all have entitlement for we are all blessed, BUT
- What have we done to increase our patience?
- What have we done to be of service to the Universe without pay?
- What have we done to break bad habits?
- What have we done to be more giving, more loving without thought to ourselves?
- What have we done to be more Holy – more like Christ?
- What good books have we read and have we learned from?
- What have we done to be deserving of this inheritance – it is ours but what have we done to be ready to receive it?
- Are we now allowing for it?
- Are we now trusting for it?
- We can certainly expect it when we know we have done our best?

It is not the deservability, we are all entitled – but what have we done for God to say, "Good work, you are now trusting and ready to receive your inheritance."

Everything we have going on in our lives at any given moment, especially what makes us huff and puff, we need for our personal growth. This is the polishing of our soul that is so necessary for our growth here on Earth. That is why we are here, to perfect the growth of our soul, not the growth of our bank account.

Who are we trusting – ourselves, our family, our husband, our wife, our employer, our government or our Creator?

Are we honoring the ONE, or those few who are showing us THE WAY to our Divine Creator? On Earth, do we know who this person is? I say honor them in any way you can, for this surely is the greatest gift we can receive – someone who is showing us THE WAY.

Of course – my beloved Jack showed me.

§

**JUNE 26, 2012**
**Nothing was ever wasted – during the war**

Me: Dear God – This morning I was remembering – for some strange reason as I was distributing the abundance of toilet tissue that I had in my hands in our house – those days during the war when my family (my mother or father for it certainly was not I) had cut newspaper into six inch squares and thread them on string above the toilet – it was our only source of paper. The septic system in England endured much. This was all we had, there was no other choice. It was all I knew, and it was all right with me. Nothing was ever wasted – during the war.

§

**JUNE 30, 2012**
**God used us**

*I was expressing to Jack how magnificent our second book was and that I could not believe we had written it.*

**Jack: We didn't. God used us because He could.**

§

**JULY 4, 2012 – 9:24 A.M.** *(and it is still a little cool)*
**A letter to Jack**

Dear Jack,
So many people have never seen what I have seen and am seeing as I speak. Visualize **Harpo** on the *Fox Feed Station* table at the back of *The House*, having just eaten one-half jar of beef baby food. He is so happy looking around. **Rozie-Bear** is under the bench of the back deck, watching the many, many birds feeding on one of the triangular feed tables you built. **Frenly** is having the best time rolling in the rocks and must have found a little catnip growing. **Lucy** is on the kitchen window sill upset about it all. This is her space, she thinks!
So many deer, so many beautiful deer and two grown does

11

loving each other, licking each other's faces, necks and bodies. Obviously they love each other. <u>I love it all</u>. Thank you for what you created here, and thank you God for eyes that see – thank you for <u>my</u> eyes.

Oh my goodness, one of the does has discovered the catnip or whatever it is and is licking (the special round stepping stone you placed in the area of the *Prosperity Garden*) exactly where **Frenly** licked. Her 'love partner' has a hurting leg and is watching **Rozie-Bear**. A couple of weeks ago I noticed this deer was limping badly, but seems to be much better today. Thank you God. <u>I love your creation, Jack</u> – <u>it allows me joy here without your physical form</u>.

I am now inside *The House* while sitting on your bar stool, writing this. I still miss you so much but love the animals deeply.

§

## SUNDAY, JULY 15, 2012 – Mercury Retrograde, Day 2
## I was sensing a heart loss. Please, please watch us

Me:  Jack – an incredible morning here:
*Harpo*, *Groucho* and *Mattie* (who never comes to *The House*), *Marie* (her twin sister) was here also, *Foxy*, *Mittens*, *Spike*, *Ebony* and *Rozie-Bear* – they were all at *The House* to see me. <u>Maybe a farewell, I don't know</u>. (I was sensing a heart loss – not easy to explain.) Fortunately, I had fed them all baby food, which is their most desired treat, I do believe. I carried *Marie* to **CAT HAVEN**, and she seemed to enjoy it thoroughly. They are all so frail in their precious little bodies but strong in spirit; I can see this clearly. Please, please watch us.
*Jack: Baby, don't doubt it for I most certainly do, and I too recognize their grateful behavior. Everything at* **CAT HAVEN** *is exactly as it should be. There is no pain, there is only gratitude, much love for you and for all you have done and still continue to do. They all know it.*
Me: Is *Sammi* with you? (*Sammi* was a short-haired black male cat

12

who preferred living outside rather than in a building, and I gave up trying to keep him inside.)

*Jack: Not yet, but he is glad you allowed him freedom.*

Me: Jack, I feel something is ending and this makes me sad.

*Jack: Honey, something is also beginning and this should make you glad. I'm glad – very much so, because your burdens will be less.*

Me: I hope I have done what God wants me to do.

*Jack: Of course you have. We both have and continue while in different dimensions.*

§

**WEDNESDAY, JULY 18, 2012 – 10:32 A.M.**
**Why am I so tired?**

Me:  Jack, I've just deep-cleaned the ice box and our pantry, and I am already so tired.  Why am I so tired from such simple things?

*Jack: It is because all you have done and you now need to rest.  The only way you rest is to feel fatigue and this is what needs to happen for you right now.  You are not sick, but you are being forced to rest – the only way that works for you.  Some people, including you in the past, had to manifest sickness, but you are no longer in that space.  The fatigue slows you down as we have had conversations on this before, it slows you down.  Be good now; accept this because it is only temporary.*

§

**JULY 24, 2012**
**Sweet tears**

Me:  Reading our second book is milking my tears.

*Jack: Sweet tears I hope.*

§

## JULY 25, 2012
### Precious moments to remember

Me:  Unshakable, unsinkable small grey kitty – *Marie*, is at our house this morning.  If she weighs a pound, I would be surprised.  She journeys from the **CAT HAVEN** building to our house with passion and joy for baby food.  My pleasure is to serve her, and I allow this to occur inside *The House*.  For me, these are precious moments to remember.  I allow her to enjoy the food she loves, and it is my pleasure to carry her back to her building.  She seems to also enjoy this 'togetherness'.  She is an angel of a kitty.

§

## JULY 29, 2012

Me: You cannot measure what I feel for you, for I love you beyond measure Jack.
*Jack: I know, and it is returned beyond measure.*

§

## MONDAY, JULY 30, 2012
### *Callie's* downtime

Me:  For five or six days last week, our precious *Callie* (who is a privileged calico house cat about 15 years old, as referenced in *Listen, I'm Still Here* – Part I, Page 64) did not eat at all.  I wore myself out tempting her with just about everything I could think of, but to no avail.

   However, Friday night I gave chicken food she had never eaten before and guess what – she ate it, and some tuna juice this morning.  To me, this was so exciting because I am not in the space of thinking it is her time to come home to you.  She is not herself, that is for sure, and she sleeps way more than usual but has gone outside a couple of nights for an hour to sit on the back patio bench, and I am rejoicing in this attempt on her part to give of her best.

Kristina came today to see all of our babies. A few cats have incredible memories (from when she worked here over six years ago) and enjoyed her voice and touch – for example: ***Betina, Crystal, Spike, Joy*** and even ***Julie***. Some of 'her' kittens (that came from her father's garage) ***Pirate, China*** and ***Lynn – Harpo, Marie, Foxy*** were a few others who had memory of her, but some had forgotten her completely; understandable, I know. For me, it was a pleasure to have her, and we both had memory recall of good times when we built the brick pathways around the buildings and other creative tasks. Kristina allowed us to take fabulous vacations, and like you – I will be forever grateful to her.

***Jack: Me too Sweetheart, and I am so glad you stay in touch.***

Me: Lou (your trim carpenter) is coming tomorrow to build a support boardwalk section over the existing boardwalk in front of our house, because we have to install a new roof. Apparently the roofers will have to traverse this area hundreds of times to carry shingles up and down, and I know what you built – so many years ago – will not support this weight. (I was carefully planning to protect the beautiful curved boardwalk that surrounds our house and getting a support walk built over to protect it.)

§

**SUNDAY, AUGUST 5, 2012**
**Our *Callie* is coming home**

Me: Several days have passed since we last talked, and I recorded it on paper. Yes, I talk to you all the time, not always do I write it down.

***Jack: I know Sweetheart. I love it. I am your constant companion.***

Me: I do hope so for these days of tremendous heat, much hard work on the land and with ailing cats, are very difficult for me. Our ***Callie*** has been so brave, so strong in her spirit, drinking water many times a day, sleeping many favorite places of her choosing and allowing special, special times on my lap and accepting my love (even this morning, she sat on the front boardwalk in the cool of the day) overflowing love, but tonight she is behind the couch on the floor in the laundry room and my interpretation is that she is ready to give up the fight for she is turning her back on the world. I so understand. I have memories of **Lucky** and others who were with us in our house and this behavior pattern. Tomorrow morning, at 7 A.M., I shall be on my way to our veterinarian, Dr. Stried, who is expecting us. He was so gracious and willing to come two days ago on Friday, but I said "no" because I want her cremated and to have her ashes next to **King's** (her lover) on the chair in the living room – I am glad I delayed this trip because **Callie** has shown tremendous grace, strength and love toward me in these two days. Selfish me; somehow I needed this. Today I am ready to allow her to come to you. Be ready to receive this special creature who I recognized just recently is so much like me – not easy to live with!

*Jack: I had no difficulty with you – none, but if you learned from her that is good.*

Me: Why I feel this transition is an ending when I know better, is difficult for me to understand in myself. This very beauty of form is hard to part with – your beauty of form still lingers with me.

*Jack: Only this 'recent' form – there were many others of which you have no recollection so allow this to pass into nothingness. Lessons learned, even from the smallest of creatures, and you are a winner. Callie is too. And yes, she adores you and will be around forever more. You can rely on that. I will bring her for a while, and then she will be on her own with King and even Ivy.*

Me: Don't let me down. Please watch us.

*Jack: Did I ever let you down?*

Me: No.

*Jack: Then let go. I am here, always here. Never doubt that.*

Me: I know you know I plan to bring **Ching** to the back portico of our house.

*Jack: That is the best idea. I am happy about it.*


## LATER – 10:07 P.M.
*Callie's* **love for me revealed**

Me:  In case you didn't know it, **Callie** has been about one hour outside this evening. She walked from the front of *The House* to the back and sat on the chair on the bench, with **Lucy** taunting her. I finally brought her in and low and behold, she went to her plate on the floor in usual fashion, and I opened a can of tuna. She actually drank some juice, her first sustenance in almost two weeks. I know, I just know she did this to please me. What a wonder to behold. How intuitive. Now I must get some sleep for I have to arise very early. Stay with me.

*Jack: Don't doubt it Baby, don't doubt it.*

§

## AUGUST 21, 2012
### Have no worry, have no fear

*It was one hour before my first media conversation on the radio. I was just **thinking** to myself. No words were spoken by me.*

*Jack: Have no worry, have no fear because God and I are here.*

§

## AUGUST 27, 2012 – 11:24 A.M.
### I am happy because I know – I am the righteousness of God

**To the World I Say**

Yes, I am happy because I know who is in charge of my life – finally I know! All of the questions I have had for so many years, especially since your move – yet again, I still see you so often when I am working around this beautiful sanctuary when you join me, flutter by my face or tell me, "That is enough." Yes, you were right by my side yesterday afternoon when I was out on the street painting the mailbox in the mid-day sun. *"That's enough,"* you said, *"That's enough for today."* You were here again this morning checking things out around the 'remembrance corner' I have created to honor you just across the driveway from

*The House* – FOR ETERNITY, I LOVE JACK; the sign says: and there are so many of 'our' little discoveries and special sweet things where the angel dust still lingers from the white rose I placed when the Archangels were here. It is so sacred.

LOVE, FAITH and PEACE are expressed on little statues – everything represented for me, my love, and for God – OUR perfect best friend. God, we are yours; show us your way.

§

**AUGUST 28, 2012**
**I love God and Jack – the same way**

Me: I love God with every fiber of my being and every cell of my DNA – I also love Jack the same way.
*Jack: And it is returned Sweetheart. It is returned exactly as it should be.*

§

# CHAPTER 3
## 2012

# NOT EVEN A HAND
# TO COMFORT ME
# – OR SO I THOUGHT
### 5th year of conversation after Jack's transition

## ILLUMINATION

*Learn to savor how good the Lord is;*
*Happy are those who take refuge in Him*

*— Psalm 34:9*

SUNDAY SEPTEMBER 2, 2012 – 8:51 P.M.

**Not even a hand to comfort me**

*(My fears before the installation of a new roof, was the invasion of so many strangers to our sacred space)*

Me: Baby, I need you to answer me tonight.

*Jack: Sweetheart, I will, I will.*

Me: I am not happy, and you know why.

*Jack: Indeed I do, you have made that perfectly clear.*

Me: Three horrific screams ten minutes ago was my alert to you.

*Jack: No, I heard you way before that.*

Me: You know it is because we have to have a new roof on *The House*, and there will be many strangers here – men I do not know, who don't speak English!

*Jack: Don't hold that against them.*

Me: They don't care about this beautiful place.

*Jack: They don't know about our beautiful place. You will be teaching them about it and what it represents. You will be opening their hearts.*

Me: Our curvaceous driveway is a problem for heavy trucks and equipment.

*Jack: Not necessarily. We have had many trucks enter our driveway when we were building and when we made improvements to our various systems. Don't worry.*

Me: I feel I don't even have a hand to hold onto to comfort me in my distress.

*Jack: Baby, you have God's hand and mine. Neither of us will let you down.*

Me: It feels like torture to me to be invaded in our sacred space.

*Jack: It will always be sacred, nothing changes that. It is God's creation through us, and everything He creates is safe. Nothing and no one will change that.*

Me: I am obviously having to trust God 'completely' to bring the right ones – who are able to do the work here.

*Jack: Exactly. Sweetheart, the right ones are coming.*

Me: I feel that the gentleman who is in charge of the roofing company can be trusted, Todd is his name.

*Jack: He most definitely can be. He admires you and what you do*

21

*and is doing his best to assure you of that.*

Me: Yes, I know. I recognized it and told him so a few days ago.

*Jack: And he was more than appreciative. His men are good men and capable men.*

Me: I guess my lesson – all by myself…

*Jack: Never all by yourself – but I understand your expression.*

Me: Is to trust God completely in His selection of helpers for this task.

*Jack: Once again – exactly. You are safe, you are safe.*

Me: <u>Jack, I will never stop missing you and your talents.</u>

*Jack: Baby, <u>I work through others you know.</u> I was happy you saw me today because I too like being acknowledged. (He was present this day in butterfly form.)*

Me: You always did.

*Jack: Yes – <u>you were the very first to give to me what I had longed for all my life: appreciation and recognition for my good deeds. You gave to me absolutely everything I had longed for and you still do.</u>*

Me: <u>We are a perfect couple.</u>

*Jack: Yes we are – <u>made by God to do God's work.</u>*

Me: Stay with me – stay with me.

*Jack: Always My Love, always.*

Me: Thank you.

*Jack: You are welcome. <u>You get yourself in the way and don't allow God's work to come to pass as He chooses. Allowing completely is where you need to be.</u> If it is not right for you, I will let you know. <u>You have felt comfort with this man you have chosen to do the work, and that is because I allowed it.</u>*

Me: Thank you God for your awesome grace.

*Jack: Good girl, give credit where it is due.*

## To the World I Say

I understand myself even more through this experience. Yes, I am still trying to do everything on my own in my own power, and it is not possible. <u>The surrender, faith and trust in God's direction are still being learned – by me.</u>

§

**SEPTEMBER 3, 2012 – 9:03 A.M.**
**I love God's chosen work for me**

Me: Oh Jack, I am so blessed through God's work. The hummingbirds – three fat ones here this morning – so playful and so thrilling to watch, and now Maria has the morning bird seed spread all over the triangular feeding tables, and the birds are too numerous to count – so happy and noisy; I bless my eyes and my ears constantly.

*Jack: Like I always say My Love, your happiness is mine.*

Me: Waves of the impossibilities that may occur tomorrow keep finding their way into my mind. (I'm still fretting about workers, vehicles and a new roof being installed.)

*Jack: Cast them out – every one – and fill the space with God's light. Everything is according to His plan and exactly as it should be. I am with you, and I am with the ones who will do the work. Have no fears Sweetheart, have no fear.*

§

**SUNDAY, SEPTEMBER 9, 2012 – 9:30 P.M.**
**On the other side, our loved ones 'know it all'!**

**A Dream**

Me: Well last night, as I told you this morning, I dreamed about some of my relatives being with me.

*Jack: And they were indeed.*

Me: My aunt Grace, who did many things when I was a child to instill goodness into me – in my dreams she definitely was present but seemed to have no interest in our first book. You told me it is because where you and she are, they 'know it all', and so our book was already known to her.

*Jack: That is quite right Sweetheart. It is of no interest because she already knows everything we said.*

Me: Jack, I believe your exact words were, "*That is because she knew it all.*"

*Jack: That's correct. Everything you do where you are is known to us over here – no surprises.*

23

Me: Here I was feeling disappointed that she rejected our book, and you told me everything we said was already known.
*Jack: Correct.*
Me: Wow!  So my mother and father know what we have done?
*Jack: **This information is available to those who choose to tune in**!*

§

**SATURDAY, SEPTEMBER 29, 2012 – <u>about</u> 9:20 P.M.**
*(Since the clock in your reading room where I sit in your chair is not working!)*

**Another raccoon invasion**

Me: I told you several hours ago that I really need your help tonight where the 'wildlife' are concerned.  You will probably remember years ago when we were invaded by small raccoons in *The Sick Bay Building* where **Ching** now lives happily.  She loves it there and enjoys both sides of this small building where she can easily crawl through the opening you made, from one side to the other.  She is fun to watch because it is the first place that she can call her own, because like me, she does not like interference.
*Jack: I know Sweetheart, and I am with you as you love her so beautifully.  She truly enjoys this time.*
*(I make it a point every day to hold **Ching**, pet her and brush her and tell her just how beautiful she is – to think she was a feral cat living in the neighbor's barn and brush piles for so long until I was able to capture her in my arms during a heavy rain.)*
Me: I enjoy her so much for she is lovely to touch.  Her fur is luxurious and she seems to like being petted – not all of the cats do.  Please keep the raccoon break-ins out of the picture tonight and in the future because the mess they create is too hard on me anymore.
*Jack: You have my undivided attention My Love for I don't like to see you work so hard.*
Me: **Ching** must be frightened, and we have to stop that.  I believe my wish just a few nights ago for the ants to move out of our house actually has come true for I have not seen one since I made my wish.

*Jack: Yes My Love. The critters will abide by your wishes also – as do I!!*

Me: You know what I have accomplished this week for the continuation of improvements on our land. The roof is beautiful and complete; the septic is clean and repaired; most of the trees have been pruned and look majestic. (This will mean less leaves to clean up in the spring.) Acorns are falling everywhere. A very nice man, named Herbert, with access to professional quality asphalt has resurfaced the entire driveway, and it looks as great as it did in 2006 when you were with me on the Earth plane, and we had spent so much money getting a new layer of asphalt laid. Cracks still appear, and this gentleman tells me they always will. It is not the surface, but it is under the asphalt that the ground moves.

*Jack: He is a good man My Love, a fair man and an appreciative man. He will always care for what you want.*

Me: I don't seem to see you as often, but yet I see a different butterfly each time – mostly around when Maria and René are here. Is it you, or am I making this up?

*Jack: Oh no, it is me and yes I may appear to you to look different because I come from a different location – from wherever my work has me situated – but yes My Love, it is me. You have good help with Maria and her son. He truly respects you and enjoys the different tasks he performs.*

Me: What about this so-called friend or helpmate you have in mind for me? I am sometimes in the space of giving up.

*Jack: Oh Sweetheart, never do that for I made a promise, and it is my heart's desire that you have comfort, but the good things are always worth waiting for. He is there, he is there, and you will blow his socks off!*

§


**LATER**

**Right timing for 'Jack's' book**

Me: I am just now, starting once again, to prepare for promoting *Little Victories*. (Jack's personal book which is about his experiences in Vietnam when he was a young Naval serviceman. His special gifts of surveying, engineering – plus he had learned the Vietnamese language and could read maps; this knowledge had him in a useful and desirable place for the C.I.A. He was the perfect pick at the perfect time to be used by our government for the dangerous and secret missions the U.S. needed to pinpoint enemy territory. He performed two secret missions but when it was realized he knew too much to be allowed to bring that information home; he was deserted and left to die alone in the U Minh forest and near the beaches of Cambodia. However, God had him in the palm of His hand and so, miraculously, he made it out of enemy territory.) I have read and proofed the self-published book one more time and am now endeavoring to find some potential avenues for publication. Help me in any ways you can.

*Jack: God will do that for us. Just know your timing is right.*

Me: <u>My love for you only grows</u> – it never diminishes.

*Jack: I know baby, I know. Mine is exactly the same. <u>IT IS GOD'S LOVE FOR EACH OTHER AS HE LOVES US</u> – <u>NO WORDS TO DESCRIBE IT.</u>*

Me: For sure. I recently found photographs of my first visit to Llano, Texas (our first date). What a beautiful day that was – the first of so many beautiful days. You were so good to me.

*Jack: Baby, I was so happy to have found you. I was at peace.*

Me: I was a little afraid for some time.

*Jack: I know. Everything with my family was a challenge, but you came through and even my mother was impressed. (Let it be known at the time that Jack and I first met, Jack's father was gravely ill with cancer, and his parents were about to move into their retirement house in Llano, Texas that Jack was remodeling for them.) It was difficult for her to reveal that in her behavior, but I know she knew you were the right one for me. Her personality never changed, but her heart knew the truth of who you were for me.*

Me: Have you seen her?

*Jack: No Sweetheart, it is not necessary for me as it is not necessary for you where your mother is concerned. Your father is around you quite often, and I witness this; yet, he and I have not crossed paths. Everything is as exactly as it should be.*

Me: You know how it was this week with little gray kitty *Marie.*

*Jack: Yes, and she does have a little more time, and yes, I believe she did hurt herself in a fall, but she is more than happy to be with you and enjoy the foods.*

Me: I know *Callie* is with you.

*Jack: Oh yes, and she and King are together again. (When on Earth together, Callie and King lived in our house and were best friends.) Ivy is around just like on Earth; she watches but keeps to herself and to me. (Let it be understood, when on Earth, Ivy was Jack's cat. I had adopted her from a PetSmart store in Round Rock. She was a Siamese, and he loved Siamese cats. I had, in a tragic accident to us, accidently run over on our curvaceous driveway, a beautiful Siamese we had at that time named Burney.) Ivy is Ivy, and allows closeness with me for sure. King and Ivy are friends in Heaven just as they were on Earth. Hamlet is a joy as are all of them. I always leave part of myself with them when I leave to do God's Will so they are never without me. It is all quite wonderful over here. Everybody gets along.*

Me: Have you seen any of your old girlfriends?

*Jack: Only one have I seen and she has great understanding and appreciation for us. Baby, you are absolutely my only interest, plus, of course, our babies. They are all my babies too.*

Me: Jack, I love you beyond words and beyond measure.

*Jack: It is returned in the same way. We are God's chosen partners – for 'eternity' it is. Never doubt.*

Words of wisdom I recently heard – 'THIS LIFE' is like a grain of sand, compared to eternity!

§

## SUNDAY, SEPTEMBER 30, 2012
### *Marie* is in Heaven now

Me: You know the outcome – our darling angel *Marie* gave up today, and I know the feeling. It is most difficult to keep going on – I was with her until the end.

*Jack: I know. I witnessed the love of both of you. All is well Sweetheart.*

§

## WEDNESDAY, OCTOBER 3, 2012
### The kind of woman a man longs for

Me: I so enjoyed a conversation today with the owner of the sign shop (where you used to purchase the construction signs you needed for our company Heart Construction and where I now purchase the signs for the property at **CAT HAVEN**). She is so nice, always so helpful and seems to have the same kind of personality that I do! We do so much and always want to do it right and have little time for ourselves. Whether or not you remember, her name is Barbara; you may remember her mother's name Pat, and Pat was the one who made the selection of font for the signage here at **CAT HAVEN**.
*Jack: You are both very special women, the kind men search for and long for. Yes, she is a lot like you and admires you also.*

§

## SUNDAY, OCTOBER 7, 2012 – 10:25 P.M.
### I am falling in love with a 15 year old

Me: Well, I am falling in love with a 15 year old boy who behaves like you – he is an Aries, again like you. His energy and appearance are like you, and I love him. His name is René, and his mother's name is Maria – our caretaker for **CAT HAVEN** now for almost seven years. His father has taught him a lot of good and helpful things where the use of tools are concerned, and yesterday he installed some hooks I had bought for the patio and annex gate, and they worked on the *Sickbay* gate also – and last night there were no break-ins to this building by raccoons. What a relief. If all is well tomorrow – Monday, I have decided to put our beautiful ***Ching*** back into this *Sickbay* space because she is making a lot of extra work for me in the portico, which I don't need right now. I cannot open the glass doors to allow air through the screens because she claws them and will not let me cut her claws. She covers unfinished food bowls with my clean carpets, and that distresses me. So, in order to have a clean portico again and be able to open the windows to let air in through the screen, I have to change her space of living. Is that okay with you?  Am I being fair?

*Jack: Sweetheart, love of my life, you are always fair, and I support your choices.  Ching knows she is loved and was happy in the Sickbay building you told me on many occasions, so put her back and allow some free time for yourself.*

Me: I think I will.  I'm still not quite right in my hands and because I moved some heavy blocks out front of the gate, my back is now hurting.  A helpmate for me is definitely needed here – a man, not a boy, so don't stop your efforts on my behalf.

*Jack: Never fear of that.  You will have it all, I have promised before and you know I am a reliable man.*

Me: By the way my friend Paul Minar, the numerologist in California, prepared the most beautiful review on our second book, *I'm Always Here*, and it sort of blew me away.  He said some remarkable things about the work, and I will use it in promoting to the publisher – I just feel that 'your' book, *Little Victories*, might need to come first because it is an election year, and our book media publicity is on hold. I'm trying very hard to accept Divine timing.

*Jack: Good girl, best girl I have ever known.  All is in Divine order.*

Me: I have stupid thoughts sometimes about getting too old to be successful – what say you on this?

*Jack: Stupid thoughts, fearful thoughts and senseless thoughts. God knows what He is doing.*

§

# CHAPTER 4
## 2012

# I MISS YOU MORE THAN EVER
### 5th year of conversation after Jack's transition

## SATURDAY, OCTOBER 13, 2012 – 8:34 P.M.
### I miss you more than ever

Me: It is Saturday night – for me the loneliest night of the week especially when your body hurts and you don't exactly know why. My thinking and my understanding goes pretty deep these days (more than most people venture), but I do not have your perfect physical form, voice and strength to comfort me, so I just go deeper and deeper yet hopefully higher and higher. I have everything, yet I don't have you.

Last night I was in a restaurant we frequented, and our favorite tables were all occupied; so, I sat in a corner and remembered! There was a young couple with a little boy and the husband was on crutches (because he had lost his right leg). My heart opened instantly to helping them and paying for their dinner, at least – which I did – and I so wanted to tell her how lucky she was (even in those circumstances) because she had her husband, and I didn't have mine. I said nothing.

My memory this Saturday night was of our first meeting in the hotel and just how much you obviously knew at that time and in that space and how little I knew about us and our lives, past and future. It is still the case because where you are now, you still know so much more than I do. I just didn't know Jack when we met, I didn't know what you knew, and I still don't.

Jack: *That's for sure. I had memory recall that swept me off my feet and when I look at you now, I am still swept off my feet. Believe me Sweetheart, there will be absolutely nothing that you long for, that you will not have.*

Me: You know the good news about Part II, our second book, *I'm Always Here.* It will be published – next year.

Jack: *Of course I know. I know it all – the when's and the where's. Don't worry your beautiful self; God has YOU in the palm of His hand. You are doing well today – resting in His love; that is what He and I want. You manifest these slow-downs for yourself because there is no other way for you to slow down.*

Me: Jack, I love what I do but this evening because my body was hurting, some of the animals were neglected by me.

Jack: *That is a joke, for not one of the animals was neglected. Not*

33

*one. You deserve a life too. We would go dancing – and how well I remember.*

Me: Jack, our city is not as beautiful as when you were here physically. It is actually to me and to some of the neighbors, disgusting – so many people and so much traffic.

*Jack: <u>Your life is in Divine Order</u> and just never forget that.*

Me: I would never have appreciated fully all you did for me, had you not moved on. Of course, I was <u>always</u> happy with you here and grateful, but the appreciation never revealed itself to such an extent until I was left alone – or seemingly so. What makes me happy now is the knowing <u>you now know</u> how grateful I am for your good deeds, your respectfulness of me and my goodness toward you. Yes, we do have a wonderful union, truly blessed. The unselfish things you still tell me blow me away.

§

## OCTOBER 14, 2012
### God's supernatural provision is ours

Me: God's supernatural provision is ours Jack.
*Jack: Sweetheart, I know and have always known.*

§

## OCTOBER 16, 2012
### I have all the help I need, I have God

Me: Jack, I have all the help I need, I have God.
*Jack: Good girl. He knows you now trust Him. Have no more worries.*

§

## OCTOBER 28, 2012 – 8:56 A.M.
### Something remarkable – 'personified unselfishness', that took my breath away

Yes, this Sunday morning I witnessed something truly remarkable – two old male cats (*Mittens* and *Spike*) that live together in the *Bunkhouse* and who endeavor to come to *The House* every morning for baby food. The weather has been extremely hot this summer and to make the journey on the black asphalt in itself is remarkable, but now for a few days it has been very cold (in the 40s) and for 15-16 year old cats to make this 400 foot journey one way, is not easy. One of the cats seems to be aging somewhat better than the other; that is *Spike*. He does not fail to show up every day and linger around the door for several hours after eating (resting on a mat) but for his roommate and friend, *Mittens*, the journey seems to be more and more of a challenge. This morning I witnessed *Spike* at the front door, and when I placed food on the plate he did not immediately eat; I was thinking he may not be feeling too well, but no, the amazing thing was – he was waiting for *Mittens,* who was taking longer to arrive and he allowed *Mittens* to eat first; he finished what *Mittens* left on the plate.

Isn't that remarkable that a cat would know his friend was coming but would need more time to get here, and he waited patiently and allowed his friend to eat first! Just think about it – *Spike* waited on and allowed his friend *Mittens* to eat before he did. I love animals so much – what lessons there are to be learned from them. This morning, this unselfish action took my breath away. I rushed to get another jar of baby food, but *Spike* was gone. I must presume he had had enough, but the sharing and allowing his friend to eat before him simply opened my heart to yet another level. If only people would behave this way more often.

§

## MONDAY, OCTOBER 29, 2012 – 10:00 P.M.
### God is ready to turn our message into a masterpiece

Me: I don't know where the above sentence came from, but it seems to make sense to me.

*Jack: Of course it makes sense because that is what will happen.*

Me: You know I have been troubled this past week with house and septic plumbing problems and have actually been frightened – however, somehow I made it through, very hard on my body with the stress factor. No one to talk to is not easy – especially for me!

*Jack: Sweetheart, I know it all. Just learn to relax a little more.*

Me: It is difficult to relax when the water well is running dry because of the leaks I have had here in the septic system, and not knowing what to do or having anyone to help me has been oh so stressful. What am I supposed to be learning – to be a plumber? I don't think so.

*Jack: You know better. Everything works for your good.*

Me: Is everything working for the good of the people on the east coast this week with this terrible storm they have named 'Sandy'?

*Jack: Believe it or not, but the answer is 'yes'.*

Me: I won't even make an attempt to discuss this because I simply do not know enough.

*Jack: Yes you really do, but it requires more than is necessary of you at this time.*

§

## NOVEMBER 12, 2012 – 7:45 A.M.
### Shopping with the Queen!

**A Dream**

In my dream, I was shopping with the Queen – in an area that I knew of but that she had not been. I had been there before, yet had to go on ahead of her to find this particular dress shop that she was seeking. The fashions were absolutely exquisite (I could design them from memory now with such unusual colors, fabrics,

designs and layers – dignified and perfect for Her Highness).
There were other people in the dressing rooms, but I had to go
ahead of the Queen to make the dress selections and find her
space in which to try clothes on. I told a couple of people that she
was the Queen, just a couple, but they didn't seem to be overly
impressed. I told the Queen that people thought she looked
familiar and had jokingly said, "Who does she think she is, the
Queen?" Her Highness smiled at this!

Me: I understand how fabric and fashion designs come through to
creative and well-established designers. I could do it myself after
dreams such as this.
*Jack: Yes, Sweetheart, that is how it happens. That is the source of*
*all artistic endeavors – God!*

## LATER THAT DAY – 11:12 P.M.
### I care so much about everything
*Jack, Jack, Jack, my beloved Jack who taught me so much and*
*continues teaching me with direction in all things, at all times, and in*
*all places and spaces.*

Jack, I have learned in the past hour so much!! I have greater
understanding in the past hour about lessons I have been working
on for years – yes, years! A beautiful book of mine that I have
read several times before now just comes alive for me, and my
understanding is so much deeper and 'fearless'. I know my
choices before you, with you in all places, are right choices. I
know now that I am safe in all places and have many from all
spaces taking care of me. I AM PART OF A GIANT NETWORK
OF LOVE EXPRESSION WITH GRATITUDE FOR MOTHER
EARTH AND WANT ONLY PEACE AND LOVE TO EXIST. I
am, with you, doing God's chosen work for sure. No doubt about
it.
   I don't have to worry about a thing. Divine timing it is and I
accept it because I am aware of the growth of 'my' soul. Yes I

am aware, and I can feel expansion by the minute. I am bursting forth with understanding and yet more love for you, for **CAT HAVEN** and its meaning, and even for me, for caring so much about everything. I WISH EVERYBODY CARED. Our babies care more than many people about each other. How sad that so many humans don't care, and their hearts are so closed to the true meaning of love ON Earth, life ON Earth, love OF Earth – GOD'S CREATION. There is so much we do not know about and are not even willing to learn about this Earth plane and the Universe that surrounds us. The fact that it is full of beautiful, God-made living things, and we fight on Earth about nothing and give no thought to the panorama of existence. We kill so much beauty in life with our angry thoughts, unkind and even wicked actions, and have no respect for God's creation. WE TAKE AND TAKE AND GIVE SO LITTLE. I feel happy with my choices.

*Jack: And so you should be My Love.*
Me: I love God's Universe and His smallest creatures.

§

**NOVEMBER 22, 2012**
**Thanksgiving Day – FOR ME**

Me: Oh Jack, my beloved forever more, I am so thankful to have *Harpo* and *Rozie-Bear* with me. Yes, they are on the back deck as I speak to you eating their favorite baby food. I am so thankful that dear sweet *Mittens* and beautiful *Spike* still come to the front of our house for treats. They have all been here today with me, and I am oh so thankful to have them. I have many other cats still, but they don't choose to come to our house – I appreciate them all because I see their fears still after so many years in this safe haven, and I love them all, but those who come just melt my heart. I AM JUST SO THANKFUL GOD CHOSE ME TO DO WHAT I DO, BECAUSE I LOVE DOING IT.

38

**5 MINUTES LATER**

Me: A small miracle – first time ever, ***Strom-boy*** is at our house eating the remaining food that others declined. (***Strom*** is a very thin totally black male cat who came to us through the neighbor and was part of a litter of feral kittens, on his land.  The name of the neighbor is "Sellstrom", and we named this cat ***Strom***).  ***Strom*** has never been at *The House* in 15 years.  At least I have never seen him here.  <u>So much to be thankful for today</u>.  Wait a minute, ***Zeppo*** is on the scene, and a fight is about to ensue.  ***Strom-boy*** fights back but runs away.  Now two plates of food are provided.  Here comes ***Rozie-Bear*** from the back of *The House* to the front, and yet another plate is placed.  I don't care how many plates of food are required, just as long as they are happy.  This is how our God responds to us.  God says, "**Be happy my Children**," as I say, "Be happy my babies."  *(GOD'S abundance is ours, and MY abundance is theirs.)*  I love God, I love my life Jack – please tell me you are here.

*Jack: Always here Sweetheart, I'm always here.*

§

**NOVEMBER 23, 2012 – 8:25 A.M.**
**First time ever – *Rose* came to me when I called**

Me: Yes, <u>our beautiful *Rose*</u> (long-haired, dark Calico named after my mother because she came to us on the day my mother transitioned. and has chosen to live apart from her cat friends and from me for her entire life.  She's unfriendly and unsociable, by choice) <u>actually walked to me in the *Playroom* for food</u>.  She was purring – she loves milk, also a very stinky fish food I found recently in a local grocery store.  <u>WHAT A THRILL FOR ME TO HAVE HER COME TO ME.  JUST HOW GOD MUST FEEL, WHEN WE COME TO HIM.</u>

§

## SUNDAY, DECEMBER 2, 2012 – 7:51 A.M.
## A man who knew God

### A Dream

This morning I woke up in the arms of a beautiful man, someone I was not familiar with; yet I knew immediately that he knew God. His arms, his touch, his voice, his words of prayer and comfort were elevating to my physical and spiritual form. Just like Jack – yet not looking just like Jack, except he was tall – very tall and I loved it. I was rejuvenated by it all – so familiar and what I long for – a man who knows God. Was it you?

*Jack: Of course. It was time for me to hold you yet again and believe me it was as magnificent for me as it was for you; yet hear me when I say your new friend will give you this feeling too, because he knows God as we both do.*

Me: Oh Jack, you know how difficult it is on this Earth realm to find people who think as we do – so few.

*Jack: I know, and that is what you are to teach. Everywhere you go, you do shine the light that you are, and people notice.*

§

# CHAPTER 5
# 2012

# I COULD HAVE BEEN BETTER,
## – I COULD HAVE DONE MORE
### 5th year of conversation after Jack's transition

## *ILLUMINATION*

*We do not have to work to be good so that God will be good to us. God is good to us because He is good.*

## DECEMBER 5, 2012 – 9:15 A.M.
### I could have been better, I could have done more

Me: I am understanding myself more and how I could have been a better wife – yes Jack, I could have. I did not understand all of your needs, and therefore I did not satisfy them.

*Jack: Baby, I didn't understand them either so how could you?*
Me: I think I am understanding the pains I feel in my body are unknown guilt. My heart is hurting, I feel shame and it is settling in my weakest body parts. I know you forgive me, I know God forgives me, and today I dedicate to forgiving myself, yet again!

*Jack: Good idea. Let's rid ourselves of hidden and unknown secrets – hidden and unknown to both of us.*
Me: "Ought not this woman be loosed"; I learned today from a TV minister.

*Jack: For sure, let that be.*
Me: When I come to you for the last time, I will be perfect Jack.

*Jack: Sweetheart, you are perfect now and for me have always been. However, I understand that if it is for you that you wish this, then let it be.*

## LATER – 8:25 P.M.
### Learning never ceases

Me: A good, comfortable day today – doing nothing but gentle things I felt needed to be done. I know you were here this cool December day because I could feel the rush of your wings as you flew past my face when I was giving extra food (seed and nuts) to the backyard wildlife this afternoon. The deer like this food in the morning and lick the tables clean very quickly.

*Jack: Yes Sweetheart, I was there and knew you would enjoy this sighting. God has me many places doing many things, which is easy over here; yet I know you're thinking and what it means to you to feel and see me. I feel and see you at all times, but MY understanding is increasing also. Sweetheart, learning never ceases.*

Me: Dear God, I wonder what I have done to be so deserving of all this goodness.

GOD: <u>Your heart is open My Child to all possibilities</u> – <u>that is what it takes to gain understanding</u>.

Me: My heart is open to you dear God, fill it with Divine ideas and your abundance.

## SUMMARY - CONCLUSION
**To the World I Say**

Yes, I could have been better as Jack's wife, I could have done more but at the time I didn't know it – only now, after 5 ½ years of thought process of my behavior do I know this. <u>Foolish to say I'm sorry when I didn't know</u> – I have learned through my beloved's physical absence and incorporating this into my life now with my animals. I am doing better; I am doing more, my heart, though with Jack, remains with me in growth. I know I live <u>in</u> this world but am not <u>of</u> it.

*Could you be doing better, could you being doing more in any of your partnerships or relationships – think about it while you still have the chance because the pain of regret when it is too late, is gut-wrenchingly debilitating. Trust me on that – and it lasts for years.*

§

**SUNDAY, DECEMBER 23, 2012 – 10:59 P.M.**
**The eve of Christmas Eve**
**My 6th Christmas without you to hold**

Me: The missing you never stops. I work and work in between the moments when I allow those fantastic memories to come through of all the Christmas' we spent together. Every one was a winner, but I think the first one was most special and the first one in this house also, wherein you allowed me to be as a child and to open the multitude of gifts you had prepared for me. How and when you bought and wrapped them will always be a mystery to me and a secret to you.

*Jack: I remember it well and the fun I had doing that. Sweetheart, you were so easy to buy for because your heart was open to appreciation. It was never the value of the gift; you were God's precious child in your acceptance of my choices for you. I remember your choices for me and how my heart opened because before you, no one, and I mean no one, had ever been so thoughtful.*

Me: Well, you had nothing; so, for me, it was really easy!

*Jack: No Sweetheart – there was always deep meaning to everything you gave and did. You opened my heart to a new level also. You still do!*

Me: Two nights ago, I had dinner with dearest Shakti at our most favorite Indian restaurant. Finally, they have removed that special wallpaper and most of the Indian urns that we knew so well. They are removing the carpet <u>we</u> walked on and putting new tile, and generally updating the look of the place - same owner, but different waiters. Remember our favorite waiter – I still do.

*Jack: I do indeed.*

§

## DECEMBER 27, 2012
### Take my pain sweet Jesus, I have work to do for you

Me: I have so much work to do and need to be free of pain. Jack, what say you on this?

*Jack: Oh Sweetheart, <u>just allow</u>. <u>It is not you but God himself who will do this for you for He knows His chosen work and the one He has chosen to do this</u>. Let go, release your trying and rejoice in the work.*

Me: <u>Come into my heart sweet Jesus, come into my heart and stay. Come into my heart sweet Jesus, and NEVER go away.</u>

*Jack: Have no fear Sweetheart; <u>He is always there for you. You make Him so welcome as you did and still do for me. I know how you feel. I know every breath you take, with doubt and without it.</u> Have no doubt My Love – <u>everything is known to God and to me. Over here, we see it all. I truly know you better now than I did</u>*

45

*when I was sharing life on Earth with you.*
*I can share more from where I am now than when I shared our bed.*
(This made me cry.) *Don't cry My Love, for me don't cry.*
Me: You know only too well I try to do everything with you in mind because I am so grateful for your creation here on Earth and choose to honor it with loving care.
*Jack: I know only too well but please – for me – don't wear yourself out.  Sit down, again and again I say, sit down.* (I was standing in the kitchen writing at the kitchen counter, whereas I usually sit in 'his chair' to write.)
Me: I love it when I feel you are so close to me that you know what I am doing.
*Jack: It is the same for me when you recognize my closeness.  I AM ALWAYS THERE BUT NOT ALL THE TIME ARE YOU AWARE, OR TAKING TIME TO BE.*
Me: I want to take a minute on my New Year Resolutions.  I think I am going to pretty much adhere to last year's.  What say you? (Every year we made and documented our personal and business resolutions to do our best for the upcoming year.)
*Jack: Read them to me yet again.  There may be some adjustments.*
Me: I think these are pretty much my life resolutions forever more.  Do you agree?
*Jack: Yes, but there may be some surprises – good ones – that I know about and will share when the time is right.*
Me: I am blessed beyond measure Jack with you as my eternal partner.
*Jack: Me too My Love, me too.  GOD IS GREAT.  I am so happy when YOU praise HIM as you so frequently do.  Those had better be tears of joy that you are shedding.*
Me: They are, because I have everything.  Just help me tonight with *Rose*.  The nights have been freezing and although there are many warm places for her to sleep, she doesn't use them.  I know she misses her love *Booger* (he had recently just simply gone away).  Like you and I, they kept each other warm and this winter, she doesn't have him.  I hurt for her.
*Jack: Don't do that – she has her places.  Not everyone can do as*

*you wish.  **Remember now, all is well and everything is exactly as it
should be.***

*I was praying and thanking God for healing all the parts of my body
that hurt and recognized I was <u>receiving healing in my mind</u>!*

**Jack: Good girl, be open to receiving healing and your Divine
abundance, God's abundance, for it is yours.  You will handle it
well.  I truly enjoyed your thought for us for Christmas.  Honoring
Llano was quite a surprise for me.  You are too wonderful for words.**
(What I had done was make a donation to the senior citizens center in
Llano, Texas in Jack's memory.  In *Listen, I'm Still Here*, Part I, it was
described as the location where Jack's parents were retiring to and
when I met Jack, he was remodeling their house.)

Me: It is my love for God and for you that directs me and yes, Llano
was a Divine awakening for me.  I will never, ever forget our time
spent there together with **Pardy**, our super dog! (**Pardy** was a golden
Labrador/Cocker Spaniel mix as mentioned in *Listen, I'm Still Here*,
Part I.)

**Jack: I see him from time to time because I make a point of it.  He is
on the land from time to time with you also.**

§

## SUNDAY, DECEMBER 30, 2012 – 8:35 P.M.
## I saw a fox this evening

Me: Just a quick note because the highlight of my day was seeing a
magnificent fox around 6 pm in the usual feeding place I have now
established across from our house in the *Gekko Feeding Area*.  It was
a good size creature and was obviously quite familiar with the food
that was about to be distributed by me.  It made me happy to know the
foxes are still here and familiar with our place.

**Jack: Sweetheart, they are always here, just like me, but you don't
always witness them.  I love to learn of your sightings and what
makes you happy.**

Me: I saw you yesterday at the *Memorial Park* when René and I were
cleaning up **Pirate's** cemetery space (**Pirate** was a short-haired black

male who had recently transitioned.) It makes so much difference to my energy level when I witness your butterfly form – please never stop.

*Jack: Don't worry My Love, this will not happen.  René is getting used to my appearance also, I can see that.*

§

**JANUARY 1, 2013 – 6:56 A.M.**
**Happy New Year Sweetheart**

Me: Later today I want to write a 'thank you' note to Paul Minar because he helps me so much.  I have joyfully packed in an envelope one of the last shirts of yours that I have kept.  It was a favorite of mine for sure, when we went western dancing.  I don't believe Paul is as large as you were, but I think this one will fit him.  I am so excited to share a part of you with someone I know will appreciate.

*Jack: You are so sweet, and yes, he will appreciate your gesture.*
Me: He gave to me a remarkable numerological reading – he said it was one of the brightest charts he had ever done!  But that is Paul – always kind.

*Jack: I can agree with that for you are bright for sure.*
Me: He said I am determined, and my brain is a "Rolls Royce" brain!
*Jack: I agree completely.*
Me: He said I was your rock and you were mine.  I had no idea I was your rock.

*Jack: Oh yes. True love and appreciation, which I had never known before you.*
Me: He said you had little karma – just patience! (That must have been why you chose me!!)

*Jack: I didn't know that.*
Me: I have none at all!  Karma, that is.
*Jack: That I believe.*
Me: Do you have anything to say to Paul?
*Jack: Heartfelt thank you for helping you as he does.  You were related before and in this life, that connection holds strong.*

**LATER**

> I feel that my Mission is about to begin, my Mission of making God loved – as I love him…and so it is!

§

## JANUARY 4, 2013
## EXPECT, ALLOW, ACCEPT

EXPECT IT.
ALLOW IT.
ACCEPT IT.


HEALING that is and God's Divine Abundance

§

## SATURDAY, JANUARY 5, 2013
### Sometimes the 'chosen' pain of loss is worse than the pain of pain

Me: Sometimes the missing your physical form just stops me in my tracks and I have to lean on something to catch my next breath. You were such an inspiration in my life and I now have to inspire myself – not easy some days. Little things like **Harpo** and **Rozie-Bear** rejecting my petting when I am already in low gear, and I don't have you to comfort me – it is very difficult Jack, and I now have so much more understanding and empathy for others. Giving up and giving in seems to be so much easier to do, but of course that will not happen. 'Your chair' is my place to recharge.

It is Saturday morning, and my next task is income tax preparation so there is not much inspiration this damp winter morning. I know Paul will call me if he receives his package today and his words will be a bright light to my day. Are you there – are you listening to my sad story this morning?

*Jack: Of course, and I am not happy to hear where you are in your thinking today. You know better and can do better, so why not do it?*

49

Me: Ok, I get it. Did I tell you our donation to the senior citizens in Llano brought lots of 'love' from the people – lots of memories for them and where and how they met their loves. There were 53 pies purchased for individuals, and a senior citizen party. The lady who handled this and who wrote a little story about our love and our meeting in Llano told me our gift was a boost to the economy of that town. How sweet! People wanted to know my name and write 'thank you's to me. I know you are happy.

*Jack: Beyond happy – ecstatic at your thoughtfulness.*

Me: Remember the magnificent buttermilk pies we shared in Llano? Remember the first pair of blue jeans I ever bought at your encouragement (was in the little country western store in Llano) because I had never worn blue jeans before I met you? (My mother didn't approve of blue jeans!! Here I was 54 years of age and still living under my mother's control.)

*Jack: Oh my, what memories for me too.*

Me: Remember the BBQ turkey we would eat in the park with our dog **Pardy**? (Witness his photo on the cover of *I'm Always Here*, Part I – a gorgeous lab/cocker mix. His fur was the color of my hair, and I still miss and love him.)

*Jack: Such simple things that we enjoyed together. Yes, My Love, I remember it all very well.*

Me: Our life was perfect, wasn't it Jack?

*Jack: It still is.*

§

## TUESDAY, JANUARY 8, 2013
### Rain, finally some rain

Me: Well, it has sprinkled most of the day, just like in London. Nothing to measure but very damp and many accidents on the roads – that is why I didn't go out today and will not go out tomorrow either. We are supposed have measureable rain tonight, like two or more inches. I hope so because the entire city and Lake District are in desperate need. The lakes are only about 30% full, can you imagine that?

*Jack: I think I did once, and I agree with you – that is not a good thing.*

Me: I am so aware of the preciousness of water, being on a well, and with so many creatures to care for, I do not abuse water at all. Everybody needs to be more careful and certainly more respectful of this precious necessity.

Jack, it's so interesting how comforting it is for me to sit in 'your chair' and talk to you. My heart relaxes and before bed, this is a good thing.

*Jack: Then talk every night. I am always available.*

Me: Right now I can hear the rain because it is a little more forceful, and I can also hear the darned old fat raccoons scampering all over the roof. This is a nightly occurrence I live with here. Let's hope the heavy rain will wash them away!

§

## TUESDAY, JANUARY 16, 2013 – 8:37 A.M.
### Finally, I realize my tears are for me

Me: It is cold, it is wet, it is winter, and I am crying. Almost six years since your transition and I finally realize <u>I am crying for me</u>. I cannot remember when someone last called me to say, "How are you?" It has been years since any of the people that we knew extended themselves to me. I give and give books and good wishes and blessings everywhere I go. Most people are grateful for a moment, but that is all.

*Jack: Sweetheart, you are in a different place and space of awareness from most people. This they know, but simply are not able to share in any way. You tread on higher ground.*

Me: <u>But I am still in the flesh and sometimes it hurts.</u>

*Jack: That is your choice of feeling because where you are in space cannot ever hurt. You live your life now in the arms of angels, and of course me. You have let go of so many fears My Love, only a few remain. Your new friend will comfort you and remove those that are lingering. All is well in your beautiful world.*

Me: So many things around this house and land to care for that I don't even understand, and simply have to muddle through.

*Jack: But you do. I hear your concerns and guide you. Believe me, all is well and you have done well. Everything is in good order.*

Me: I don't know what to do next with either of our books to get them to the next level.

*Jack: You have Divine ideas and are working with them. There is time.*

Me: What about your book, *Little Victories*. I have concern here.

*Jack: <u>Never have concern. God is in charge, and He will direct you. Trust that Sweetheart.</u> You have been so good about the trusting, and I am pleased with you as is God. Enjoy yourself and the resting is most beneficial now for I see that is what you are doing. Have no guilt.*

Me: Thank you so much My Love. When my heart feels this level of peace, I know you are here.

*Jack: Always and always. <u>I'm always here.</u>*

## \SAME DAY – 10:19 P.M.

Me: Because I have rested more than usual for the day has been too cold to work outside, I have seen more television than usual. Wow, what a mess out there! People in Washington just don't seem to be able to compromise their ideas and as a result, there is a constant battle of anger. No one gives in, even a little. Our poor President must be out of his mind with duress. His ideas seem fair, but Congress is not. <u>I try to believe God has everyone exactly where they are supposed to be for us to learn from when we, as people, have elected them to office</u>. What say you to this?

*Jack: <u>Stay in the love vibration Sweetheart and no harm will befall you. Trust God, and that He knows what He's doing and who should be in charge – HE IS</u>.*

Me: I love you once again beyond measure for you keep my heart at peace when it is frequently ready to break.

§

## WEDNESDAY, JANUARY 17, 2013 – 9:27 A.M.
### Being used by Jack

Me: This morning I was recalling in my mind a previously untold experience which had happened about 5 weeks earlier, actually it was December 11, 2012 when I had met a younger man who had charm for me and who had infused me with many compliments, including the fact that I was 'beautiful'! Of course this had held my attention, and I followed up to check on his artistic endeavors at a local art exhibit he had told me about. And at that time, I met his wife, as well as witnessed his work!! I was revealing to Jack this particular morning, that in almost 25 years of our being together, this was the only thing he had ever done that I did not like. I asked him, "Why did you do this? Arrange for me to meet a tall, handsome man who moved my heart, and was married?"

*Jack: To wake you up.*

Me: To what?

*Jack: The beauty of you.*

Me: As you see me?

*Jack: No, as God sees you.*

*(I actually believe Jack used this man, who probably had no idea what he was saying, but he used him to get to me because he knew there was attraction.)*

§

## JANUARY 21, 2013
### What I want

Me: I want to live my life in pursuit of an ideal – that makes me different.

*Jack: You are already there.*

Me: I hope that is you responding and not me.

*Jack: Of course. You are not that swift in your responses. Sorry, but it's true.* (This is so true because I think, think and think before I respond.)

§

## FEBRUARY 5, 2013 – 10:35 P.M.
### 'Thank You's' galore

Me: Well, yesterday I picked up a large manila envelope at our mailbox, and it was full and I mean full (well over 50) of 'Thank You's' from the citizens of Llano thanking for the pies we bought them at Christmas. So many 'shut-in souls', beautiful people who have no family (like me), who have lost their partners (like me) and who appreciate small gestures (like me). I cried with joy as I read some of their precious notes. Some only signed their names on 'Thank You' cards, but it was wonderful and something I certainly never expected.

*Jack: Sweetheart, when you tell me this kind of story, my heart is overjoyed at your thoughtfulness.*

Me: The lady who seems to be in charge has a birthday one day before mine, and I am able to love myself through her because she handles things so well, does exactly what I would do. I see this beauty in her and now recognize it in myself. You know I don't give open invitations to visit here, but I extended an invitation to her because I would enjoy meeting her and having her experience **CAT HAVEN** and the work you accomplished. Maybe this will happen one day.

*Jack: Good girl for she certainly is deserving of your company and don't give up hope.*

Me: I know you know I have been working for a few days on an article for a magazine. I am proud of what comes through me.

*Jack: You should be. You write very well because it is from your soul.*

Me: Jack, I don't really know what I'm doing, I just keep doing.

*Jack: Yes you do know, because you have God's prompting and hopefully mine.*

§

## FEBRUARY 7, 2013 – MID MORNING
## My new space for being

It was mid-morning on this day when I had once again read the article that I had been working on for a magazine. I was thanking God for my clear thinking and my level of understanding and said, "Thank you God." I heard...

**GOD: Aaaah, it is My work My Child!**
Me: (I was gasping at the answer.) Jack, am I imagining this?
*Jack: No Baby, you are in touch.*

## SAME DAY

*I declared this morning that, for me, 'the cart before the horse' would bring about a Producer/Director for a movie, <u>before</u> the sale of so many books. I had just been told by a Marketing official, with the Publishing House, that my thinking was out of line. I allowed his ideas to slip into nothingness, and I put my ideas first.*

## To the World I Say

<u>I have found a new place to be</u> – a place and space of <u>not caring</u>, <u>not fretting</u> and <u>not worrying</u>, <u>and I just love it</u>. <u>I love being there</u>. I find myself laughing to myself a lot. I feel safe, I feel comforted, and so 'knowing' that my hopes and wishes are coming true – no matter what people of authority may say or suggest. **I KNOW ALL IS WELL FOR ME.** I have been here before in this space, but not for a long time. It seems my animals know this space because they don't worry. <u>I am their god and never let them down</u>. <u>I know my God will not let me down either</u>. It is very simple. My heart is at peace, and Jack is happy.

*Jack: I most certainly am, and have waited a long time it seems to hear this from you. <u>God can now do his work completely through you because He knows you are ready for His abundance.</u> Baby, it is yours.*
Me: Thank you. I know God's abundance is mine and not my limited funds. All is well for me and our animals.

## To the World I Say

My timing is God's timing, and I now know it and accept it. I am finally growing up.

*Jack: Oh boy, are you?  This makes both God and me happy, very happy.*
Me: I so want to make you happy Jack, happy with me, because <u>you</u> did so much for <u>my</u> happiness.
*Jack: Done deal Baby, done deal.*

§

## FEBRUARY 13, 2013
## My elegant life

## To the World I Say

I may have lived in bomb shelters, but I had a very elegant life, a very profound teaching life.  My home life, although disciplined, was full of 'how to behave' lessons; my school life (an all-girls' school) had me knowing how a young lady should care for herself and her body – no temptations and uniforms I would suppose helped.  My early childhood, though restricted by the war – I did have some glorious times through uncles with positions of authority in famous hotels.  For example, one uncle was an Executive Chef at the Dorchester Hotel in London (opposite to Hyde Park) and a second was an Executive with the Nestle chocolate company.  If I'm not mistaken, he had something to do with the perfection of what we now know as the chocolate drop. He hand-made all the children in the family incredible chocolate Easter eggs at Easter time, filled with handmade chocolates. On birthdays, the children were invited to the Dorchester Hotel to celebrate and enjoy 'Knickerbocker Glories' (very tall ice cream sundaes) and sipped tea in the elegant tea shop where the waitresses, at that time, wore black dresses, white aprons and starched, pleated accessories on their head, which resembled crowns.

My mother's constant judgment and criticism –I realize deep down had a profound affect on my life which sometimes 'now' seems 'positive'. I see the difference in the way I was raised and the way girls are raised these days. Although a lot of my behavior was obviously based on fear – fear of doing wrong, fear of not acting like a lady, fear of offending my parents – I believe sometimes that fear was good for me. When I think about it now, my mother did work for the highest protocol, and so it is no wonder she behaved the way she did, and expected the same from me.

§

**FEBRUARY 15, 2013 – 11:15 A.M.**
**I am glad I hear Jack's promptings**

Me: Yes, I heard your prompting this morning. And yes, as you know I went to *Ching's* house, her place and space where she has lived alone now of her choosing, summer and winter, for almost three years. I believe I heard you tell me 'enough is enough' and so, she will never be alone again until she joins you, neither will I. What I did was to go and retrieve this beautiful Siamese who had for years lived as a feral cat in spaces and places that had been provided in the woods, but she did not want to be secured in a building with others. About three years ago, I had managed to rescue her during a series of heavy rains when I literally secured her in a comfortable space where she has chosen to live alone. It was now time for her to live with me in our house, and this is what Jack was telling me to do. She has been on my lap for almost 24 hours, and the experience for me is reminiscent of my *Brandy*. (In whose memory **CAT HAVEN** was built. *Brandy* was a long-haired Calico, and more details about her are outlined in *Listen, I'm Still Here* – Part I, our first book.) I might add that *Ching's* claws are in and out of my robe which is such a comfort for me, and I believe for her also, for she hardly moves except in circles to get more comfortable. *Brandy* loved being held and in blankets with me, and so too does *Ching*. A complete circle of

57

events, and if I close my eyes, it could so easily be **Brandy;** yet again, 30 years ago when we slept together on the floor in my little house that became 'our' first shared home together, that was Jack's and mine. I am happy, I am grateful, and I feel both of this from **Ching.** It was a great idea you had, and I am glad I hear your promptings.

§

## MONDAY, FEBRUARY 18, 2013 – MID MORNING
### *Ching* is an absolute angel

Me: Wow, wowee – **Ching** is an absolute angel. Three nights we have slept together in my newest zero-gravity arm chair. She knows where her food and box are (outside in the portico you built) and gets up in the night quite frequently to eat and drink and then returns to my 'stomach'. It is wonderful. She follows me everywhere in our house, and in fact, in the kitchen where I had been standing and making my breakfast, she was sitting on my feet! I could not believe it. Now it is a little after 1 P.M.; Maria (my helper) just left, and there you were in regal form, huge and well-rested I could tell as you flew between us, Maria and I that is. It is almost 80 degrees today, so you decided to enjoy this day with us. Oh my goodness, my heart feels free.
About 30 minutes ago, I heard from my lovely publishing gal that there is an opportunity for a radio interview on Wednesday, in Washington State, and of course, I said yes. I know Spirit or you will tell me what to say.
*Jack: Baby, don't ever worry about that. I am happy for you, and of course I knew about it before you. I love knowing!*
Me: I love the fact that you do because I don't want any secrets between us. When we first met, I had endeavored to keep a few things unknown to you.
*Jack: Yes, and I remember it well, and I didn't like it – but those were your fences. No fences now.*
Me: That's for sure and none wanted. **Ching** is now asleep on the floor in the living room in her large, deep cat bed which I brought up from her former space. I know she is happy, and I certainly am.

It was the best idea you had.  She is so intelligent.  The only thing she does not like is getting her claws cut – I think of the ten she has, I have managed to snip six.  So far she has been very good, but she does have a couple of scratching places that I don't like.  It was so good to see you, your butterfly form, for it has been a long time for me.

*Jack: Not for me!*

**SAME DAY – 9:30 P.M.**

Me: *Ching* is so intelligent; she is almost like a 'little person'.  How she watches me, my every move.  How she sits by me and looks at my face.  Just to think she was a feral kitty we made friends with and suspected she was *Mama Two's* baby (a second mother cat that we had observed on the land many years ago) from a second litter she had here, and now *Ching* is sharing 'your chair' with me – it is quite remarkable without doubt.

*Jack: You are happy, and I'm happy.*

Me: Remember, three years ago how she was missing, and the Archangels revived her – well now I am reviving her.

*Jack: Sweetheart, you revived her many times.  She knows of your love and is endeavoring to return it.*

Me: She is accomplishing her mission as I am hopefully accomplishing mine.

**LATER – 9:40 P.M.**

Me: For almost 30 minutes now, I have been laughing with joy.  *Ching* is sitting on my book on my lap while I am sitting in 'your chair'.  Can you believe that?  Our little feral cat is in your chair.  She is stretching across my book, so it is impossible for me to read.  I am allowing her time while I collect myself and my joy.  She is so human in her behavior; it is stunning – originally and for years feral, she had been sleeping in the neighbor's barn or brush pile – alone, now she is on the floor curled up at my feet, sleeping.  I'm going to go to prepare to sleep for the night with full expectation of her company.  Thank you.  (Just for the record, because it is so important to make note of since as a kitten, *Ching* has been a loner – never had access to the many toys our other cats had). This evening, she is chasing a golf ball that I had found out on the property – she hits it and chases it <u>like a kitten</u> (in human years, she is 70-80 years old, 11-12 in cat years). It is so wonderful to see.

*Jack: I am so glad you tell me of this, for this I did not know.*

§

## TUESDAY, FEBRUARY 26, 2013
### It could not be better

Me: Sweetheart, something to report that is unique to us. Exactly one year ago today, our first book, *Listen, I'm Still Here*, went to press, and today, our second book, *I'm Always Here*, goes to press also. The point is we have a second book with the publishing house – isn't that remarkable?

*Jack: Yes, Sweetheart, it is, and it is thanks to you and your efforts. Yes, <u>I AM ALWAYS HERE BUT UNLESS YOU LISTEN AND ARE WITH ME, WE GO NOWHERE</u>. We are indeed a unique couple and yes, it is God's work we do. Have no fear; the light will shine on your path to God's abundance.*

Me: Yes Jack, I believe that – I really do.

*Jack: <u>That is all He wants my love</u>, the <u>trust in Him</u>, and <u>I see quite clearly you have now accepted your part in the plan</u>. Good girl. God is most pleased with you, and so am I. It could not be better at this time.*

§

## MONDAY, MARCH 4, 2013
### Hummingbirds are coming

Me: 10:41 A.M. and with an audience of *Harpo* and *Rozie-Bear* I have put the hummingbird syrup out for the first time this year. They are due in five days or so, and I want to be sure I am ready for them.

*Jack: Good girl. You are truly so good and so thoughtful.*

Me: Jack, I didn't understand anything about hummingbirds until I

60

met you. You introduced me to so many wonderful things.

*Jack: You too Sweetie, you too.*

Me: Do you know our second book is in the hands of the printers as I speak to you today? Isn't that fantastic?

*Jack: It most certainly is. The young lady who is helping you is certainly a blessing.*

Me: How do you think I should present Part II to the public? Should I use the media approach in the same way or should it be different?

*Jack: I think different so that we have the best of both worlds, so-to-speak.*

Me: I don't know if we have made any sales at all, but somehow I don't worry about it.

*Jack: Good, because you are not supposed to worry. God knows what He is doing.*

§

## MARCH 5, 2013
### Rewards for our work

*I was explaining to Jack about Mollie Harrison's call from the publishing company and the support we were going to receive from Hay House for our second book, I'm Always Here – Part II.*

*Jack: I KNOW, I KNOW, I KNOW.*

### To the World I Say

Today was the absolute best day of my life since the transition of my beloved husband, Jack Farley, because today was huge in my rewards for our dedicated work. My most favorite publisher and my most favorite person (Mollie Harrison) with that publisher, is going to support me with the promotion of our second book, *I'm Always Here*. This beauty (our book) is already on the Internet on the Balboa website and positioned as #3 on the New Book releases. Wow! And just who do I think I am? I am what I am, and I do what I do without even really knowing what that is. I AM GOD'S INSTRUMENT WITH A MESSAGE TO IMPART

TO THOSE WHO ARE WILLING TO LISTEN AND READY TO LEARN WHAT IS POSSIBLE – COMMUNICATION WITH OUR DECEASED LOVED ONES. I now have professional people available to help which is something I have wanted for six years but never dreamed I would have. It has been God and Jack and me – not a bad trio, but we are ready to receive help. Thank you Mollie – dear sweet Mollie Harrison for your presence in our lives. You will light the way I know to what God expects for His work.

§

## MARCH 6, 2013 – 8:55 A.M.
## My faith account is full

Me: Yes Jack, I love God, I love me and most certainly love you and your teachings. Today my faith account is full to the brim. I have professed my faith in God's plan for six years now, every day – and every day I see clearly that this was the right thing to do. No matter how difficult, no matter how tired I have been, no matter how much pain I have experienced in my body and how low my hope was at times, there was always, always that little ray of light shining through, and somehow my heart knew – of course with your promptings, that everything was good for me. After my conversation yesterday with the Hay House publishing representative, I now have it confirmed – yes, my faith account is starting to overflow.

*Jack: I am so happy for you and proud of you My Love. Hopefully your feeling my presence was of help. I was there beside you, always there Sweetheart, always doing my best to help you see that light. All is well for you and the babies, no more doubt. God has you in His hands, and you will never fall again – done deal.*

§

## MARCH 12, 2013
### I know who is in charge

Me: Jack, I know you know – however lately I am able to tell you with joy in my heart – today I received the very first published paperback copy of our second book, *I'm Always Here*. It is quite beautiful. I have not examined it totally, but at first glance it looks good. Wow! We are most definitely published authors now. It is getting to be a habit. I just enjoy talking to you so much.
*Jack: Me too Sweetheart, me too.*
Me: Your book, *Little Victories*, will never be forgotten, but I know you understand I have to pursue work with the publishing house for 'our' books for a while. It is an opportunity I cannot let go of.
*Jack: Boy do I understand that and most certainly wish for you to pursue it. Everything happens in right timing, we both know that. Not to worry or fret because you know who is in charge now, without question.*

§

## MARCH 14, 2013
### I'm not happy when our babies don't come home to me

Me: You know that for two mornings and two nights now, our *Gus* has not shown his little face (Gus is a short-haired gray Tabby that we adopted 12 or 13 years ago. Not a very sociable cat but made friends with a female named *Rose*.) I know enough to know cats do go away for several days at times – we have experienced that on many occasions, and if as you declare *Gus* is not with you; then perhaps he is on a personal journey. He was here two days ago and looking good. My sorrow is for *Rose*. Our dear sweet *Rose* was looking for him this morning. She lost her true love about five to six months ago (*Booger*), and has recently bonded with *Gus* for companionship, comfort and warmth. She was looking all over for him this morning and could not eat. My heart bleeds for her. See what you can do to get him back for a little longer. They are about the same age (*Rose* and *Gus*).

Also, *Linen* (the youngest we have – one of the kittens from about four years ago) is not around either. Two males, both friends together and friends of *Rose* – help us out.

*Jack: I will certainly do my best, but neither of the missing boy cats are here. Don't fret Sweetheart, as I always say – everything is as it should be.*

Me: But what about our *Rose*?

*Jack: Rose is doing what Rose does well – taking care of herself.*

Me: I know, because she has never circulated with others – sort of like me – but she does love those she selects. *Booger* and she were just like us, so close. I keep thinking that maybe *Gus* and *Linen* have gone off exploring together; they were friends. Keep me posted.

*Jack: Never fear Baby. I am with all of you, especially Rose and you.*

§

**MARCH 15, 2013**
**Still no *Gus* or *Linen***

Me: Rose cried this morning, and I have never heard *Rose* cry.

*Jack: It was good for her. It was a breakthrough of her emotions. Rose now has feelings which she has never shown before. Rose loves you because she finally understands your goodness toward her. Everything is good Baby, everything.*

§

**SUNDAY, MARCH 17, 2013**
**Linen is back home at CAT HAVEN**

Me: This morning *Linen* was home. No *Gus*, but it was nice to see *Linen* and hear his cry. I choose to believe that *Linen* went wherever his friend *Gus* went and stayed with him while he made his transition – a good deed from a little animal who does not do many good things. However, this is my choice of belief. Our *Gus* was not alone, and I assume he is with you now.

*Jack: Yes, he came over two days ago. Linen was a good boy, and I*

*believe that too.*
Me: I am going through all the barriers as if they didn't exist.
*Jack: Because for you, they don't.*

*P.S. A ray of sunshine for this evening around 6 P.M. – one hummingbird appeared and looked a little bit like **Sentry** – you will remember how we named this soldier-like hummingbird because of his posture – a good sight for me of the end of a trying day.*

§

## MARCH 26, 2013
## My personal growth

### A Dream

I was very high up on a skyscraper that was being built of concrete, solid blocks on top of solid blocks – many pinnacles. It was extremely high; I was somewhat afraid of the height, for it seemed to be moving, swaying in the wind a little. I was afraid of the height, the movement, and it was cold. I believe you were there Jack because I was explaining my feelings and that I wanted to go down 'to pee'. It seemed to be okay with you. Somehow I got down and when I did, I found an old camera of ours and was taking some photographs for you of how it looked down here in an area you knew of and in fact, had created. The camera didn't work, but you assured me that was okay.

I went back to this enormous building and saw that it was just about complete, and I couldn't believe it, and that I had been part of it way up on top.

I recognized that the expanse of this construction from down here was huge. It seemed that in the beginning of our ascent, we had a helper. He (she or they) had left a note as to their whereabouts. I didn't quite understand the note they left or where they were or who they were, but word from you lead me to believe it didn't matter.

*Jack: Baby, it didn't matter. We have always had unknown help, yet known help. This leap of faith by you is monumental. You are on solid ground, and yes My Love of all life and its times – everything, absolutely <u>EVERYTHING FOR AND BY US</u> – and <u>FOR EVERYONE – IS AS IT SHOULD BE</u>. Like it or not. <u>GOD'S PLAN REIGNS SUPREME AND NO MATTER WHAT YOU SEE, WHAT DISASTERS SEEM TO APPEAR, IT IS AS GOD IS CHOOSING TO SHAKE HIS PEOPLE INTO UNDERSTANDING</u>. Your understanding has been enormous these past days, about us, about yourself and your son – yes your son and why he chose you the best a mother could be. You extended yourself and gave to him everything a mother should give. He searches still from his father. He knows of his errors and lives with them himself. Let go. All is well; you are in God's hands and His many angels.*

§

## SUNDAY, MARCH 31, 2013 – 8:55 P.M.
### The sweetness of you is missed beyond words

Me: Six years of learning – and I have certainly learned a lot, but obviously not enough yet to live a weekend of memory of your transition without allowing myself to feel pain. My choice, obviously, and certainly not yours, but somehow the sweetness of you is missed beyond words. I never knew a man could be so sweet, so kind, so thoughtful, and so unselfish for you were all of this and so much more. I miss that. I've only got me, and I am none of this in excess! I irritate myself – and you have my permission to laugh at this – but I do. Maybe I won't have a friend until I can be more kind to myself.

*Jack: He is there My Love, but preparing himself for you because his soul knows he needs to be ready!*

Me: Are you just saying this?

*Jack: Not at all. You will have understanding once he comes on the scene.*

Me: So many beautiful old songs written when I was very young keep strumming through my mind – they used to write really good songs about love and feelings and touch. Not so anymore. "The very thought of you My Love," brings an abundance of pleasure for me.

*Jack: Likewise Sweetheart, likewise.*

Me: I know you see how well our **Ching** is doing and how happy she is with me in our house. She makes me happy too with her obedience and appreciation. She really is no trouble and enjoys sleeping on me in my new chair. She is good company.

*Jack: I know and am happy you heard my prompting.*

Me: I am pleased to think she is not alone in her last days, and I hope I won't be either.

*Jack: It is planned and it is perfect, and you will be cared for.*

Me: Part of me wants to talk to you about the marketing of our second book, yet it is so confusing and seemingly out of sequence to me that I shall say nothing, do nothing until I feel things are in right order.

*Jack: Great, good idea. There's plenty of time for you.*

Me: I hope so because it is very, very expensive and is basically over in a flash.

*Jack: Do what your heart tells you to do, and I don't have to concern myself with your choice. You know what God is telling you.*

Me: I am going to be talking on a couple of radio shows this month.

*Jack: Yes I know, and you will be great at that.*

Me: I have to trust Spirit will give me my answers to the questions I will be asked.

*Jack: You know that is so. I am so proud of you and your accomplishments. I always knew of your potential, but you did not. You are flying Baby, My Love is flying.*

Me: Because of you.

*Jack: No, because of your trust and your faith in God's love and direction. As I told you recently, He has you in the palm of His hand, and He is smiling.*

Me: That is a lovely thought.

*Jack: It is true.*

Me: Oh Jack, I'm trying so hard to see beauty here without you.

*Jack: Look within yourself. You do what you do Baby because it is what God wants. Your heart loves doing it. It is what you and I were born to do. It is our soul's purpose, and your rewards will come on Earth and in Heaven. I see so much more than you, so trust me. GOD'S REWARDS FOR US ARE EVERYWHERE – NOT IN OUR BANK ACCOUNT. THERE IS NOTHING SECURE ON EARTH, ESPECIALLY IN A BANK. Sweetheart, you don't have to be sad because I am still here – always here. I never leave you; it is just the difference in this new arrangement of our time together, but believe me – I am still with you, every moment.*

Me: I have just read through the entire book, *Heal Your Body*, and conclude I am having a hard time letting go of what is now over. You and I will never, ever be over, but I have to adjust to a different level of loving and having you with me. Help me.

*Jack: I am ready and willing to do anything you ask of me. OUR LOVE IS THE HIGHEST AND DEEPEST KIND OF LOVE TWO SOULS COULD BATHE IN. IT WILL NEVER END BUT NEEDS TO BE CURBED SO THAT FOR YOU, LIFE CAN CONTINUE AND BE BEAUTIFUL. You deserve this, and I want this for you, and I know you need and want it too. Let go Sweetheart, pretend you are swimming, and God and I are holding you. You know you will never sink or fall. Enjoy yourself with our support. Please My Darling, for me, enjoy yourself. It's all I want for I know I have your heart and I will never, ever leave you. Your happiness is my happiness, so let's have a good time. For me, have a good time so that I do too. It's very simple, and it's what I want. Make new memories for us. I have everyone that you and I had and don't doubt that.*

§

**APRIL 3, 2013**
**Where I live**

Me: I live in your arms all day.
*Jack: No Baby, God's arms.*

§

68

## APRIL 7, 2013
## I see the reflection of me through the cats

Dear Jack,

My reflection – the reflection of me, myself, I see so clearly in two cats, my last two cats at our house. One lives inside and the other lives outside.

These two most precious of God's creatures are reflecting back to me by their characteristics, the best and the worst parts of my Gemini Cancerian character. ***Ching*** reflects the sweetness of me, the huggable lovable side of me, the disciplined perfectionism of me, the appreciativeness of me, the flexibility of me, the humorous side of me, the speediness of me and the respectfulness of me – just about all of my qualities, while ***Lucy*** reflects the difficult side of me: I won't eat this and I won't eat that, especially when you want me to. I want to be loved under my conditions and in my timing – when I want but not necessarily when you want. The elusiveness of me, touch me today but maybe not tomorrow.

*Jack: Yes, My Love, that is you and for me, that was no problem. Variety is the spice of life, and you kept me on my toes. You still do, and I am happy with you.*

Me: I can easily handle ***Ching's*** behavior because it is what I want in everything, but ***Lucy*** drives me crazy! I understand that she out-pictures everything I need to accept and love about myself and about others.

*Jack: Right on!*

Me: God certainly moves in mysterious ways to teach us.

*Jack: **And yes My Love, it is up to us to recognize His ways. They are all around us, at all times and in all places.***

Me: I am a pain in the you know what Jack, and I am so blessed that you love me.

*Jack: Easy Baby, it is easy.*

Me: Ours was and still is a uniquely magnificent relationship. I am glad I was honest from the very beginning because I knew I was not easy. I told you I needed a masterful companion, someone with complete control of himself because they would have to handle me.

You were able to do this.  You were the best on Earth, and I knew it.
And maybe, just maybe, I am putting forth that special effort while
you are in Heaven to reach you, because I know I have to make up to
you.  I want to make up to you more than you will ever know.
*Jack: Not necessary, but do as you wish if it completes you.*

§

## APRIL 9, 2013
Me: God, I am so grateful for this beautiful place in which I live.  I
don't know what I did to deserve it.
**GOD: It is not what you did My Child, but what you will do.**

§

## WEDNESDAY, APRIL 10, 2013
**Finally, we have printer proofs of our second book,** *I'm Always Here*

Me: I am astounded at the wisdom you exchange with me.
Remarkable words of truth.  I have great difficulty believing that this
all came through me to the paper.  Yes, I know I hear you, and I write
what you say – but when I read it, it is indescribable.  My heart is
more peaceful this evening that the finished product can be approved
and now circulated.  I found out today that there will be a filmmaker
on our property in a few weeks.  Think about that for me, and tell me
your thoughts.
*Jack: Sweetheart, this is just up your alley – you will enjoy
planning, escorting and you will do very well.*
Me: Lots of work to be done by Maria and I in these next few weeks
because this is the messy time of the year for the land.
*Jack: You will accomplish that to perfection – your standard – but
don't hurt yourself to please anyone but yourself.  I will give you
energy if you pace yourself.*
Me: Thank you – I needed that assurance.  This is a magnificent place,
and I think the filmmaker will enjoy his day here, so many places to
choose from.

§

## MONDAY, APRIL 22, 2013
### Today you touched me, and I knew it

Me: <u>Yes, you touched me through another</u> – <u>another man, a tall man, and I saw you through his eyes when I was in a favorite lumber store today looking to replace a tool you had purchased six years ago that was now needing to be replaced</u>. I had the tool in my hand, and this beautiful tall gentleman saw my predicament, recognized through your prompting that he needed to lend a hand. He did, gently, purposely and with kindness in his eyes and before he left, <u>he touched me! My word, that was you, touching my left shoulder as you would do</u>. Thank you Sweetheart, thank you for showing yourself through another beautiful man – a tall man, a very pure man I could recognize easily. <u>You were able to work through him because he was willing</u>. <u>It was quite a lovely experience, and I saw it all unfolding before my eyes</u>. A 'fabulous' experience.

§

## TUESDAY, APRIL 23, 2013
### Our first radio interview and I loved it

Me: I don't have to tell you how I prepared myself physically and mentally today to do God's work and to receive God's words. It was so much fun. I think the gentleman did an outstanding job! He was prepared and seemed interested in what we had to say.

*Jack: You were great, and I was there. He was interested because he was in the space of understanding what we have to say. I was proud and happy too. You respond to this type of situation very well – much better than I would have. I can handle it well from here, but was never as good as you are when I was there, get it!! Good job. There will be many more opportunities, and I want you to accept them all.*

**Today:** A doe and a crow together face to face today on the *Gekko Feeding Table*, quite a sight!

§

## SUNDAY, APRIL 28, 2013
## Once again, I am in 'your chair'. I love it here

Me: Well, you know how difficult the landscaping work is at this time of the year. So much pollen, so many leaves and strange weeds to clean up. I spent several hours this weekend uncovering what you and I created so many years ago here with the beautiful rocks we placed and the beautiful rocks that were, and still are immovable. Unless I show René what to do to find this magnificence, it will be buried forever more, and I could not stand for that to be – here. Our creation is so lovely, and I want it to remain as 'we' created.

*Jack: Good girl. Sweet girl, my wonderful wife, you are revealing in your own words some of what I appreciated in your personality – the perfection and protection of God's beauty and how you would uncover it and enhance it. You are still joy and my delight. Sweetheart, I watch you work, and I feel my delight within my soul as you rediscover. Believe me when I say I don't miss a thing. When you are thrilled, so am I. TELL EVERYONE WE ALL FEEL THE JOYS THAT YOU FEEL. IT IS NO DIFFERENT HERE FROM WHEN WE WERE THERE – YOUR HAPPINESS IS OURS.*

*(For the record, I had been on the pity potty complaining about my aches and pains and not feeling deservability of a new friend.)*

*Jack: Come on now, that is not what it is all about, and you know that better than anyone. This man I am still working on has had great difficulty himself and will be so relieved to find you and your wisdom and inner beauty, that you will sweep him off his feet, and he will be a great comfort to you. This I want so much also.*

*Honey, it is God's timing, and we all have to wait on that – even I do! I love you more than ever – and like you, the love increases with your every breath.*

*It seems to me that you know exactly what your problems are, and how foolish you are to think this way. Honey, God knows what He is doing, and as you wrote last week – everything is already a done deal. God has already made the selections and done the work. Your problem is still not trusting this*.

Me: Thank you. I feel you.

*Jack: Of course.*

Me: I still miss you.

*Jack: Not necessary Sweetheart for I am in you, and you are in me. I love the memory recall of our trips, and the Isle of Wight. Yes, I smile at the simplest thing we did. For me, it was more than extraordinary to be in England with you, yet again. Yes, My Love, your soul had intense memory of our departure from each other in another life. Neither one of us recognized this until much later.*

> *Reference Page 59, Listen, I'm Still Here – Part I*
>
> *...experienced a past life where sadness brought me to my knees. I could feel myself waving goodbye to a ship and sensed most definitely that it was Jack aboard the ship and that we were saying sweet but painful farewells. It happened at the same place in two consecutive years when I put my foot on a certain spot on the island. There are no words to describe it; I just buckled from the sense of the loss and felt distinctly like it was the loss of my love, Jack.*

Me: Sometimes I do feel that you are in me – so close and it is good.

*Jack: It most certainly is. Whenever you have this realization, I tune in immediately. My wife feels me, and that for me is good also.*

Me: So I can still make life better for you?

*Jack: Absolutely, in many ways. Be happy, and know I am there.*

§

**APRIL 30, 2013**

**I'm hurting myself to please God, and I know that is not right**

Me: Just to be sure you are hearing me and my sad story today – I'm going to repeat myself yet again. Jack, I am hurting myself to please God, and I know only too well that is not what He wants.

*Jack: Don't go any further. That's for sure, and so, gets yourself off the pity potty because I won't join you. Never would and never will – so there! Get used to it!*

73

Me: Nobody, absolutely nobody is responding to me. Nobody returns my calls, and I feel so alone and then I remember your words of many occasions which assures me I am not – alone that is, and today, I realized yet again that there is only you and God and when I allow it – YOU BOTH RESPOND TO ME.

*Jack: Right on!!*

Me: I think my lesson yet reinforced is that I am not to trust people, but trust God.

*Jack: Yes, that is all you have to do.*

Me: I am absolutely wearing myself out taking care of this place – which this evening I realize I LOVE doing, so 'the Mission' for me is great! 'The Message' – well, I certainly LOVE hearing from you and our dearest friend God, but the message I don't care too much about relaying because the majority of people have no interest. It's like swimming against the current, and I don't have the energy for that anymore.

*Jack: Again Sweetheart, you don't have to do that part of it; allow God to come in and take over. LET GO AND LET GOD. It is the trusting that you sometimes grasp and then let go of. Yes Sweetheart, you have done the creative work, you have allowed God to use you. You have created something unique and beautiful, and now LET HIM HAVE IT AND DO WITH IT WHAT HE CHOOSES.*

Me: Jack, right before my eyes are the words of a minister, "You don't have to make things work. All you have to do is to Pray, Hear His Instructions and Obey."

*Jack: Perfect, absolutely perfect. Yes My Love, you are in Divine Order.*

Me: The words continue, "Remember that the Lord your God, He is God in heaven above and in earth beneath, and He will go before you and prepare the way."

*Jack: That is it, that is all there is to it. YOU HAVE NOT BEEN ALLOWING GOD TO PREPARE THE WAY. YOU HAVE BEEN TRYING TO DO THIS YOURSELF.*

Me: So right, and I am absolutely worn out. My health is suffering. I see that absolutely everything I had thought to be reliable down here, such as the few people in my life, are not reliable at all – they are not meant to be. GOD IS THE ONLY RELIABLE SOURCE FOR US, and I am being forced into this awareness.

*Jack: I don't like the word 'force', but I understand where you are coming from. Baby, **GOD IS ALL THERE IS**.*

Me: Jack, in my dreams tonight please visit, please bring Guardian Angels, Archangels and remove my imagined sickness.

*Jack: Done deal Sweetheart, but please ACCEPT IT. **No resistance, no disbelief – we cannot work when there is doubt. Let go Sweetheart, I know you can. I witnessed it so many times. IT IS SO SWEET FOR ME WHEN YOU LET GO**.*

Me: I want to be sweet for you.

*Jack: **Then do this simple thing God and I ask. Forgive, forgive, and forgive everyone** – including yourself, for this you sometimes forget to do.*

Me: Oh Jack, my beloved husband and best friend, what would I ever do without you?

*Jack: Don't even go there for it will never be. Always, always – it is you and me.*

§

### TUESDAY, MAY 7, 2013 – 11:07 P.M.
### Our beloved *China* went to heaven today

Me: Our beloved *China* (a chocolate brown Siamese) left this earth plane today lying in her soft bed on pink satin covered with pink lace. What a joy for me to recognize your promptings this evening as I left our house to feed our babies, almost one hour earlier than usual – and what a gift that was for me. When I reached the *Playhouse* to check on *China* (who has been ailing for a couple of days now), she was lying under a table, and I believe gave her last cry as I entered – that familiar cry of hers – which was loud and hopefully of gratitude recognizing "Mama was there for her". I most certainly was. I promptly moved her into her soft bed, placed her on the pink satin we always use for the girl cats and lay my loving hands on her as she drew her last few breaths. Yes I cried, of course I did. I had so many wonderful memories of her as a kitten, when we took her and her brother *Pirate* in. At that time, she was almost white with little brown tips on her ears and tail. As time went by and as she grew, her coat changed to this marvelous milk chocolate and then dark chocolate color. She was beautiful. You will remember her brother *Pirate* (jet black) had made his transition before Christmas after a somewhat painful few days with an ulcerated leg. They were wonderful brother and sister friends. If he was ever out of her sight, she would cry loudly for him. Do you remember?

*Jack: Yes Sweetheart, I remember. Pirate is here and knows she is coming.*

Me: The breaking apart of friendships with people or animals seems to be the same for me, it hurts, yet the comfort follows whenever I realize we will all be together again. <u>Our reunion</u> will be breathtaking.

*Jack: Yes, Sweetheart, it will and I promise I will have all our children, our family that we created, together again, when you come home. <u>Take your time</u>. Everyone is happy here, and we want you to be happy there.*

Me: I love *China*, and I always will.

*Jack: Me too Sweetheart, me too.*

Me: Tomorrow Maria and I will bury her in our cemetery on our land. This I like – she will always be here in spirit – her brother is already in the cemetery, and she will be near him.

*Jack: Your ideas are beyond perfect. I will be close to you this night.*

Me: P.S. for your information, Michele has put a photograph of you and I on my new phone so whenever I turn it on, there we are.

*Jack: That sounds just like you and what you would want. Thank you to Michele.*

§

**MAY 18, 2013**
**To the World I Say**

> Take my doubt, heavenly Father/Mother God
> I am willing to let my heart and soul be filled only with love and faith.
> I give up all doubt – in Jesus name.

§

## MAY 21, 2013
### It may be *Happy's* time to come home

Me: I am concerned about **Happy-Boy** in the *Ruffhouse* for I think
he had some kind of stroke. His eyes are off balance, and he is more
scared than usual. Stay with him. If you could ask God to take him
tonight, it would be helpful, because tomorrow will be difficult for
him and for me. You know how fearful he has always been and does
not like to be touched. I know he will fight me if I attempt to take
him to the vet, and he could seriously hurt me. I have the cemetery
ready because I know I have several aging cats who will not be here
much longer now. All of them (**Mattie, Marie, Ebony** and **Foxy**) still
eat very well for I don't count the cost of the best foods that they like.
*Jack: Good girl. I support you in that area and want for you to*
*make them happy. I would do the same thing.*
Me: If you could convince God that taking **Happy** tonight would be
most helpful, especially to me, because I do fear getting hurt, and he
could do that.
*Jack: I will do my best, but it is Happy's timing we have to honor.*
*I love you for all your efforts. You are the best My Sweet, the very*
*best.*
Me: We will be on our way to Dr. Stried in the morning to have
**Happy** put to sleep. Watch over us in the traffic. I have the cemetery
prepared; be with me.
*Jack: I will My Love, I promise I will.*

§

## MAY 22, 2013
### *Happy's* timing

Me: **Happy** made a choice <u>not</u> to go with me this morning to the vet.
This evening he is hiding.
*Jack: You will find him as he chooses to be. Don't worry – <u>his life,</u>*
*<u>like our life, is choice.</u>*

§

## MAY 23, 2013
### *Happy* is on his way to heaven today

Me: A miraculous happening today because Maria comforted *Happy* and together we got him in the carry cage. Dr. Stried put him to sleep, and now he is buried in our cemetery where we first started burying cats. I know you know where.

§

## JUNE 6, 2013
### My husband was <u>never</u> late for anything!

*I was disappointed at one of the publishing house writers who had made changes to my language in a marketing press release when they wrote of, "my late husband." I said out loud:*

Me: My husband was not late for anything!
*Jack: And neither are you.*

§

## SATURDAY, JUNE 8, 2013 – 9:05 A.M.
### Our priceless *Mittens*

Me: Wow, Jack, what a magnificent sight to look out of the kitchen window and see *Mittens*, who lives in *The Village*, and I don't believe I have ever seen him at our house, let alone at the back of *The House* sitting on the bench where *Harpo* and *Rozie-Bear* usually sit. Maria had just filled the bird bath with fresh water, and he was standing on the huge rock beside the feeder on his tiptoes drinking! <u>Miracle #1</u>: he was at our house.

 <u>Miracle #2</u>: he did not run away when I went outside and in fact, when I called him to me on the deck, he came right over. He is not looking his best because he seems to have a moisture deficiency in his mouth which makes the cleaning of himself difficult. He is not able to lick his fur completely due to the lack of saliva and as a result, his fur is in tuffs – one-half clean so to speak and the other sticking up all over. Whenever I usually try to touch him or brush him, he doesn't allow this. Well, this morning it was different. He allowed me to

work on him for about 15 minutes, and I know it hurt. I was gentle as I could be, but I know it hurt. I ended up with a box full of fur, and he seemed so happy when I was able to sweep the brush down the center of his back from his neck to his tail. I was happy too. He had eaten one-half jar of baby food in the process, and again, was thirsty. At this time I poured him a huge bowl of water, and he drank half of it.

Miracle #3: he allowed and seemed to enjoy my face next to his, and I was able to kiss his head – something that has never happened before because he is a scaredy-cat and always runs away. Today was different.

Miracle #4: he is sitting on the back bench next to *Rozie-Bear* – who lives, in yet, another house in *The Village*, and they were both peaceful. The hummingbirds and many other birds are back and forth to the feeders, and *Mittens* is watching it all. He sat on my lap for just a minute, but it was the first time in about 12 years or more. Our priceless *Mittens* was magnificent today.

Beautiful *Oreo*, *Spike*, *Zeppo* and *Sooty* are outside the front of *The House*, all comfortable and very peaceful. I am happy. My life would be absolutely nothing without these animals.

This place is magnificent Jack. The deer are presently eating the bird seed on the tables while the squirrels are running up and down the trees to the same tables. Birds are surrounding the bird bath where *Mittens* was recently perched. I love this place – it is heaven on Earth for me, and the only thing missing is you.

*Jack: Never fear Sweetie, I am seeing exactly what you see.*
Me: I am going to add one thing that I just became aware of – *Harpo* was not at our house this morning which is very unusual.

§

## MONDAY, JUNE 10, 2013
### More miracles from *Mittens*

This morning *Mittens* was once again sitting on the back bench and looked so pleased to see me. I, once again, took every brush and comb we have and tried to clean his fur up. He was very accepting of the tugging and even purred. He liked the attention, and I enjoyed doing it. His body is one half perfect across his back, but his tummy needs serious attention. He was a little resistant to my pulling tufts of dry fur out, so progress this morning was slow, but I will do my best every opportunity I get. He has turned out to be very appreciative and showing his love and appreciation for me with love bites.

Not such a good report from *Harpo*. I wondered why he had not come to the back deck on Saturday for baby food, but since he liked to climb on high buildings I did not concern myself too much until late this morning, when I saw him in *The Playhouse* stationary, nursing a swollen, left-front paw. He was hurt obviously. I picked him up, rescued him and took him to the **CAT HAVEN** building and put him in one of the individual cubicles. He was so thirsty he drank an entire bowl of water. I think that he was unable to get onto the table where the water bowl was placed in his own building. He also consumed an entire jar of baby food without stopping to breathe. I was glad I had everything he needed. He could not place his left-front paw on the ground – it was bent under his body, and he dragged it. I placed a call to our dear doctor friend, Dr. Stried, who told me two things – this past week he had retired from his clinic but that he would take care of our animals no matter what. This was very satisfying for me. I gave a report on *Harpo* and this morning, Monday the 10th, he came early to check *Harpo* out and review *Strom's* painful throat problem. *Harpo* had apparently injured his shoulder in some way (possibly jumping down from a high building) resulting in his inability to place his left paw on the floor. All he could do was to drag it. What I need is a miracle Jack to help him, and I'm asking for this tonight. Dr. Stried is getting me pain medicine for both cats. I am not without support for the animals, and this is most valuable to me.

§

## WEDNESDAY, JUNE 12, 2013 – 9:27 P.M.
## Thank you God for the priviledge of our beloved *Harpo*

*Harpo was one of a family of five kittens; we first saw him with his brothers,*
***Groucho** and **Zeppo**, running around the floor of the veterinarian's office when*
*he was just a wee kitten. It was Easter time, and we could not bear to think of*
*these three beautiful little guys being alone in a cage during the Easter season*
*and so, we adopted them. They had two sisters, **Ebony** and **Oreo**, who had*
*found other homes for one year but then were returned to the vet's office, and we*
*were asked if we would like to take them when they were one year old. We said*
*yes, and this completed the family of five. They were all absolutely exquisite*
*animals and so well-behaved, but **Harpo** was without question – the most*
*evolved cat we have ever had. He was like a little child, and then a young man;*
*strange but so true.*

Jack, I know you will agree with me about *Harpo* being a
priviledge to have in our loving space for so many years. He gave
and gave of himself in so many unusual and evolved ways. He
was so intuitive, so respectful and in tune with 'our' pain – my
pain from time to time when you were here on earth also, and we
had lost other kitties. He knew I was hurting always and would
present himself in loving ways to comfort. Well, since Saturday
when we recognized he was hurt until last night, Tuesday, he
was limited in every way. He simply could not walk. He was a
darling boy and somehow got himself into the litter box (a small
low one I had placed in the cubicle for him in **CAT HAVEN**), but
he could not stand to drink or eat, so of course, I held the bowl or
plate up to his beautiful face. I did this all through the day and
through the night because he needed the water. I noticed during
the day on Tuesday that his foot was smelling unhealthy, thinking
perhaps he had been bitten, but this morning when I alerted Dr.
Stried to please come for I felt it was time; he said that the foot
had gangrene, and then I knew I had made the right decision.   I
was with him, holding him, loving him from 7 A.M. until 8:30
A.M. when the doctor came. I also had asked René to please
be present because *Harpo* and René had become close friends.
*Harpo* sought out René whenever he was working on the land and

went to him expecting petting, and he always allowed René to lift him up and put him inside his building. This was a gift they gave to each other. René held this little beauty's leg so that the doctor could put the needle in his vein, and I held his head and back. *Harpo* was not alone in his last minutes – he was surrounded by loving energy, for Maria was there too. I had taken him to his familiar building last night so that his friends could see what was happening to him and say good bye. I know they knew what was happening – I know it. This morning I lay his body in his blue satin bed for a short while so that all his friends could see him and say a final farewell. I so believe these little guys know more and care more about what is going on than we ever give them credit for.

Maria, René and I buried him in the beautiful cemetery we are creating. His name is on the stone that covers him, and his brothers (*Groucho* and *Zeppo*) will be on either side of him when the time is right. One sister, *Ebony*, is already close by, and the space for *Oreo* has been selected. This little family of five will be together in this place while their spirits are in heaven with you.

*Jack: Yes My Love, I have witnessed your strength and your love this day and like never before. And yes, when you suspected my presence in the* **CAT HAVEN** *building this morning, I was there – Harpo knew it, and he welcomed me by looking up. We were there together as always. I know you feel alone because you don't see me but Sweetheart, I promise you I am there for everything.*

Me: I think I saw your butterfly form one day this week, and it was such an elevation to my spirit. Please let yourself be seen more because I so need it.

Lou did his usual fabulous work here today repairing major building damage that had been done by the raccoons. They are so destructive, but he made things look like new again. He is a lovely friend to me, and I truly enjoy his presence.

*Jack: It is mutual I do believe, because you are kindred souls.*

§

**JUNE 14, 2013 – 9:02 A.M.**
**Rich rewards – our *Rozie-Bear* knows he is loved**

Riches, riches – rich rewards for me. Our *Rozie-Bear* knows he is loved; he finally accepts it.

For almost a month now, *Rozie-Bear* (who was rescued outside Rosie's Mexican Restaurant many years ago, as outlined in our first book, *Listen, I'm Still Here* – Part I) has come to the back deck. Today he was here and enjoyed his favorite foods and drank a huge bowl of water I had placed for him inside the empty fountain. He allowed me to love him, pet him for almost 15 minutes wherein I wept because I knew he was finally accepting love, my love, therefore God's love. His time might be close at hand, but I am happy he accepted love and didn't resist. He surrendered. We are both better off for this, and happy.

§

**JUNE 15, 2013**
**Wow, stupid me**

Me: Can I really be so stupid, so insecure, so unevolved? I see clearly today why I am still here on this Earth plane – I have so much yet to learn – to 'master'. Yes I see it clearly, and no I am not ready for Heaven or for you Jack, who are growing in leaps and bounds in Heaven.

You know only too well what happened today. I was on my feet for over 12-14 hours working physically hard – washing wood decks and boardwalks and marble patios, and tending to cats and their wellbeing and yes, my body was tired – and I do mean tired – well-earned fatigue doing honest work to care for this beautiful sanctuary and its inhabitants. The raccoons are rampant – at least three mamas and nine babies that I can count. They are so belligerent, demanding and a bit frightening. However, I keep putting the dog and cat foods out, and I open cans of food and fruits I no longer like and feed them plenty. Yet in the middle of the day when I was finishing with the deck cleaning and feeling good about how well I had done things and that God had provided enough water to wash the wood decks well, I came in to eat and when I looked outside, I saw the most magnificent sight.

There were two huge, and I mean huge butterflies (wing span over three inches) flying in unison, and I knew it was you. I ran outside, and I saw both of you in perfect harmony and immediately thought (understand this was my warped thinking) that here you were with your new lady friend, and I was debilitated with jealousy. Yes, I was so jealous, I was stifled and stationary. How could you bring your new lady to our house!! I was so upset; I couldn't breathe for a few seconds. I asked you who this was and was it a lady, and I 'think' you said no – but my emotions was so overpowering, I couldn't hear you and continued my own discourse of thinking. YOU HAD A NEW FRIEND IN HEAVEN, AND HERE ON EARTH I DIDN'T! I felt wounded for seconds, maybe minutes – I don't know. I managed to walk inside and then laughed my head off at my own stupidity. You would never do this. You would never flaunt a new female partner before me, you just would not. So why did I think you would? I am so stupid.

*Jack: Baby, not so. I can actually smile myself when I think of your reaction. Not only would I never do this, but it would never happen. How could it? You were, you are and you will always will be my one true love who continues to grow onward and upward. Sweetheart, you are my everything, and your friend Paul was oh so right when he told you later this evening for you, that I was with a high power, and I was choosing to boast that you were my lady.*

Me: After Paul's incredible perception this evening (I had felt none of this at the time I witnessed your presence), it made so much sense, and I could see your growth because both of you were the same size, dimension and in unison. I can see why I did not yet have a lovely friend, because I am still learning how to behave.

Paul is absolutely the best friend and brother to me, and I so appreciate his wisdom and help. Take care of him this week during his surgery on his right eye.

*Jack: I promise I will be around him. His right eye indicates he needs to view himself (his male aspect) with more in-depth clarity.*

Me: I am genuinely sorry I doubted the meaning of your appearance. I ask forgiveness.

*Jack: Not necessary.*

§

## JUNE 16, 2013 – 8:22 A.M.
### How incredible is nature

**To the World I Say**

It is a good day when I see the hummingbirds, and today I can see they are here together with dozens and dozens of birds feeding on the triangular tables you made – one of which is exactly where you placed it at the back of our house leaning against the huge oak tree. Even the deer cannot get close to the tables to eat right now. What a sight and what an inspiration! Our work is appreciated. Less than five minutes later, I simply had to go out and give them more. I simply had to.

Dear God, I love what I do and I love what I see, and it is all so satisfying to me.

Keep my body strong so that I can continue your work.

## LATER THAT MORNING – 9:14 A.M.

Now there are squirrels on one half of the table and birds on the other half. It is all so beautiful, far better than anything seen on the television.

How incredible are the ears, the hearing of the animals, especially the deer. Whenever I place dry dog and cat foods on the plastic plates at the feeding stations for the growling mama raccoons and their babies, within minutes the deer are streaming down the driveway, across the land from the north and south to this treat because they hear the crunchy foods hitting the plastic plates. How intuitive they are – they hear, they know what is going on, and they come.

It is hard work maintaining **CAT HAVEN** but such rewarding work, so peaceful and so satisfying. I am grateful God chose this work for me.

Me: I love you Jack.
*Jack: I know, but love God more because it is from Him that all good things flow.*
Me: You made a good one God when you made my Jack.

**GOD: <u>He made himself My Child</u>.**
*(I recognized immediately it is God who creates us, and we are all equal, but what we do with this creation is up to us. <u>We do make ourselves</u>.)*

§

# CHAPTER 6
# 2013

# I HAVE CHOSEN TO TAKE THE TOLL ROAD TO HEAVEN
## – I HAVE CHOSEN TO PAY THE PRICE!
### 6th year of conversation after Jack's transition

## ILLUMINATION

*The present moment is all we are assured of*
*– so it is holy and irreplaceable.*
*We must do our best right NOW –*
*to assure our destiny – our mission is fulfilled.*

*— Einstein*

**MONDAY, JUNE 24, 2013 – 8:35 P.M.!**
**I have chosen to take the Toll Road to Heaven – I have chosen to pay the price!**

**To the World I Say**

The 'High Road' can be a lonely road; yet, with few others on the Toll Road, we pay the price to drive in safety, to enjoy limited traffic, an uninterrupted view and we reach our desired destination safely. What could be better? Yes, this I recognize is the choice I have made for the growth of my heart and soul.

I am learning so much on my journey with God because I am willing to learn and wish others were willing also.

So many have chosen a life that is stifling, restricting and limiting because they are afraid (the FEAR), to give up their comfort zone of existence. Hearts are closed to change, and the growth of the soul is therefore hampered – sad, but rampant on this Earth plane. They have chosen the road to nowhere!

- ❖ Ears are closed to what is possible. They do not listen.
- ❖ Eyes are closed to what is possible. They do not see.
- ❖ Hearts are closed to new ideas that take them out of their comfort zone into a new and elevated level of existence. UNDERSTANDING AND LOVE – WHERE THERE IS NO FEAR.

I know of this elevated level of existence. My beloved Jack taught me when he was here in physical form, and he continues to teach me where he now is – on the 'other side'.

In this Earth realm, I find myself now viewed somewhat as a space alien – because of my thinking and writing, combined with Jack's teaching from his new realm of existence – I appear to be someone from another planet that no one can relate to. I am still me, but used by God at His choosing – an instrument He can work through because I am willing to be used.

I GIVE our beautiful books and get open eyes at the gift, and seemingly eager hearts, but I see it is only my wish for them to learn – not their wish for themselves.

So if you appear to have interest, so if you are open to listening, so if you are open to learning what is possible when our hearts open to a new level of understanding and if you really want to be the best that you can be – YOU HAVE TO PAY THE PRICE. There are so many closed minds and therefore, closed hearts. It is a choice others are making, but not me.

I have chosen the Toll Road. I am paying the price and am traveling fast without restriction. I remain open for I know what the possibilities are. Thank you God.

**GOD: It is your choice My Child, the right choice.**

§

# CHAPTER 7
# 2013

## I DID NOT KNOW 'HOW' TO LOVE AS YOU DID
### – NOW I DO
6th year of conversation after Jack's transition

## ILLUMINATION

*Try not to become a man of success,*
*but a man of value.*

*— Einstein*

**JUNE 29, 2013 – 8:24 A.M.**

**Jack, I did not know HOW to love as you did when you were with me on Earth, now you are in heaven – I DO**

Me: When you were on the Earth plane, I <u>know</u> now that you really did love me more than I loved you; <u>THE ONLY REASON I DIDN'T LOVE MORE IS BECAUSE I DIDN'T KNOW HOW.</u>

Only now through these wonderful animals, *Ching* in particular, am I learning HOW. There is absolutely nothing I would not do to make her life better, happier and I remember distinctly when you asked me if there was anything else <u>YOU could do to make ME happier</u> – I said, "Learn to dance!" (This made us both happier together.) I talk to and listen to *Ching* with the same question. Of course I do this with all of the cats – they were lost, abandoned, unwanted until us, but most of them (like people) are on the empty gauge because they simply do not know how to love, to give love or to receive love – FEAR gets in the way. There are those (animals), the famous few – *Harpo, Groucho*, *Bitsy*, *Rozie-Bear*, *Foxy*, *Oreo*, *Mittens, Marie, Mattie, Zeppo* and *Spike*, who have all spiritually grown so much because they have been <u>open to giving and receiving</u>. Let us not forget our *Belle* – 'our' last rescued cat together, who has always been grateful and now shows her appreciation to me every day. She cannot get enough love and at times, I feel bad that I don't have time or energy in this 106 degree heat at 9 P.M. to give more than I do.

> <u>If we don't know how – we cannot give.</u>
> <u>If we are not willing to learn – we do not grow.</u>
> <u>If we are not open to receiving – it passes us by in this or any area.</u>
> <u>If we don't seek – we simply do not find.</u>

You know where I am in my gratitude to God for bringing me you. I wonder how many other people have that fragrance of perfect love close by and cannot even smell the sweetness. *Ching* is sweet fragrance for me, and I bathe in her essence and say thank you to God. <u>Every day I am opening my heart to this new level of awareness, understanding and loving</u>.

Yes, My Beloved, I now <u>am</u> more than I was when you enveloped my physical form with your strong arms; however, I feel and hear you from Heaven – I had awakened from a dream and heard the timely phrase 'lovely brown eyes, lovely long legs, lovely strong arms to squeeze you'. You had all of these attributes.

Some of our cats have been with me now for 12-13 years and are still as fearful and closed and not allowing even a head pet! Can you imagine? Others are or have come around and relish the attention I extend. I SEE SO CLEARLY THAT PEOPLE AND ANIMALS ARE EXACTLY THE SAME. WHEN ENVELOPED WITH FEAR, THE LOVE PASSES THEM BY. Sad isn't it – especially for people? FEAR PREVENTS GROWTH, ACCEPTANCE AND THE WILLINGNESS TO SURRENDER TO GOD'S LOVE.

I think I heard you say yet again – "*God is ready to turn our message into a masterpiece!*"

*Jack: You did, because it is so. Yes, My Love, there are many among us who do not know how to love, and our writings give them a chance to learn. EVERYTHING IS GOD, ABSOLUTELY EVERYTHING AND WHEN AWARE OF THAT THE TRUST IS MAGNIFIED, THE DOUBT AND QUESTIONING CEASES, WE ARE IN THE LOVE VIBRATION, AND ALL IS WELL. You are there Sweetheart, and all is well.*

Me: I'm so sorry Jack that I didn't give you everything you wanted.

*Jack: I didn't need everything I wanted. I had you, and that was all I needed.*

§

**JULY 1, 2013 8:31 A.M.**

**There is no difference in soul growth between brothers (animals or human)**

*What a glorious morning – so much activity, birds, and yet more birds swarming the feeding tables; so many hummingbirds also around the feeders under the patio cover (they move so fast), and there in the midst of this activity sitting on the back bench is our dear sweet **Mittens**. He has already eaten half a jar of baby food and a saucer of his favorite cat milk, and he still looks toward the kitchen window in case I have more.*

§

94

## JULY 4, 2013 – 11:04 A.M.
### I'm proud that I can hear you

Me: A joyful day today – once again, so many hummingbirds. I cannot count them. In one swoop, I saw about six or seven (for this location, this is an abundance). I am refilling their feeders just about every day, and I wondered why – now I know. This hummingbird dance is a priceless show – spectacular. They are positively swarming today – maybe they have on other days, but today (July 4, 2013) I am endeavoring to take it a little easier, and so I am focused on their activities. We have so many beautiful guests. They are happy, and so am I.

*Jack: Me too Sweetheart. I love this kind of news because I know the peace it brings to your heart. Remember now, WE share your heart, and I feel exactly what it feels.*

Me: I'm starting to worry about our *Ching*. She is not eating very much, and she sleeps all the time – hardly walks around our house like she did even a week ago.

*Jack: Please Sweetheart, she is doing what she is supposed to do. It is God's hand that is upon her, and she is safe and happy in The House with you. She is no longer alone – which I might add she wanted for many of her years, but now she loves to be with you. Your care is all that is required for God is in charge of it all.*

Me: I know, but I am oh so glad I hear your promptings. The one you gave for me to retrieve *Ching* from the space she was living in was loud and clear. I'm actually proud that I can hear you.

*Jack: Think how I feel that you can also.*

§

## JULY 6, 2013
### No regrets

TRUE LOVE – I AM LEARNING – IS GIVING UNTIL YOU ARE ABSOLUTELY TURNED INSIDE OUT TO PLEASE – PEOPLE OR ANIMALS, OR WHATEVER YOU DO. Since the animals are my family that is how I choose to give and have absolutely no regrets. To realize, when there are no more chances to please the person or animal you love so much and who have left the physical plane, is extremely painful. Sometimes more painful that the loss to your life. I've had a few regrets and want that no more. I would rather turn myself inside out and know I did everything I possibly could have to make the life of my love in any form, happier.

§

# CHAPTER 8
# 2013

*'DARLING' CHING* (A SILVER AND GOLD SIAMESE)
**– FULFILLED HER MISSION
TO 'COMFORT ME'**

6th year of conversation after Jack's transition

## ILLUMINATION

### God's power shown through His creatures
Is it by your understanding that the hawk soars stretching his wings
toward the south?
Is it by your command that the eagle mounts up
and makes its nest on high?
On the cliff he dwells and lodges,
upon the rocky crag – an inaccessible place
where he spies out food.
His eyes see it from afar.
His young ones also suck up blood,
and where the slain are, there is he.

*- Job 39:26*

§

God, oh God – you are a wondrous God.
I know none of this but am witness,
to some of this.

**JULY 2013**
**Many are oblivious to nature**

**To the World I Say**

The wondrous works of God, all that He has created, and yet so many people spend so much time oblivious to nature. What are they teaching their children?  We humans take and take, yet again God's beautiful land, and build and build yet more for ourselves without giving thought to the homes that have been destroyed – of God's creatures.  Seldom do we provide for the now homeless ones.

On 'our' small parcel of land, Jack and I have given it back to God.  This is our contribution to making the world a better place.  I see for myself that 'our' Mission is being accomplished through all the displaced animals who find their way to **CAT HAVEN**.  There is LOVE in this place and space.  There is Divine abundance of all they need to meet their needs.  There always will be, long after me, for God says, "**The right ones are coming**," to continue 'our' loving work.

§

## JULY 2013
## 'DARLING' *CHING*
## How we met (in the late 90's)

On a job site, in the country, at a somewhat abandoned house that Jack was remodeling, he found her mother (an exquisite long-haired Calico) and we named her **Mama Two** because at the time of the trapping, this mother had with her one very small, very pretty light gray Calico we named **Foxy**. **Mama Two** (our second mother cat to arrive on our land) and **Foxy** had lived for some time in a space of nothing except a dirty fish pond and what was available for catching to eat in the way of fish, or birds. This mama cat produced several litters of kittens on our land and as hard as we tried, we never could trap her, until one lucky year when we were able to do just that and to get her spayed. These litters would show up in various places and surprise us because all of the cats that we were aware of, had been neutered. It was after the last catch, so-to-speak, when I one day witnessed as I was cleaning – this very beautiful silver and gold Siamese was eating food in one of the dog houses we had strategically placed for cats who did not want to go in any of the houses we had built. I made effort to watch and to time this appearance every day for several days and recognized the times that she would show up. I let my voice become known to her and my appearance. One day, I was waiting for her sitting down on the deck where I knew she would be, and guess what – she 'came to me'. This was the beginning of the friendship which lasted 14-15 years.

For several years, she was happy with this lifestyle coming at least two times a day to eat in a dogloo and walking through the long grass back and forth from the neighbor's barn to us (a lengthy walk in long grass). We, of course, introduced canned food very soon after our first meeting; I would somehow get flea medication on her because she loved to be petted, but not to be picked up. We made three or four different safe sleeping places for her on the land with hay and blankets, for the winters, and she used them all. It was not until after Jack's transition when the first 'picking up' of her occurred and the first placement inside a very warm and comfortable house began, and for a short while it was accepted. When, to me (later on), it was obvious that the journey from the neighbor's barn to our house was too much for her to make every day in the rain and heat, and when she would not show up on time, that I again whisked her up to the luxury in which she spent the last years of her life. The last months were in our house, actually doing things she would have done as a kitten, had we been aware of her existence or been able to catch her. In these last months, she played with cat toys, ran after tinkling cat balls and responded to feathers. She lived on my lap in fake fur and ate baby food to her heart's content – and mine. She was loved beyond belief; she knew it and she responded with love beyond belief. Her eyes, her face and tongue were exquisite gifts she gave! She had a sweet fragrance that I bathed in. On her head, she had a light spot in her fur (like touched by God's hand) – as did her mother and several of her kin – including *Foxy*, and we recognized this when Jack was here physically. We knew who her mother was and somehow, she had escaped the initial trapping of her mother's babies, but what a joy we finally found in her – or she found in us – a perfect reunion.

*Jack: Baby, she was as happy there as she is here and will be available to greet you when the time is right.*

Me: She knew love Jack, and she returned it.

## CHING

**A sweet fragrance to my life with a definite purpose to 'comfort me'**

She is keeping my heart open to what is really meaningful in life. She is more than beautiful, more than well behaved, more than attentive, more than intelligent – she is doing her job, and it is remarkable to watch how to she comforts me, follows me, sits at my feet or on my body as much as I allow – for when I am eating, I do say 'no'.

§

**FRIDAY, JULY 5, 2013 – 4:19 A.M.**
***Ching* was looking for me 'in our house' – imagine that!**

Me: Well, we made it through another harrowing (to me) Fourth of July and the neighborhood fireworks. Public displays of fireworks over the lakes I understand and have enjoyed, but neighborhood people who disturb everybody in the wee hours of the morning I don't, I simply don't! It is so thoughtless disturbing others, including all the animals who run from their homes in fear. Anyhow, we are here this morning, and I was up well before 5 A.M. to let our ***Ching*** into our house from her residence, which is now in the back house portico. When I first saw her and the way she was sleeping on the cool cotton sheets, I honestly thought she was already with you – sleeping so peacefully! Lucky me for yet another day I have her beauty to adore.

*Jack: She is with both of us wherever she is my love and never forget that. WE ARE ONE and wherever you are, I am.*
Me: She did not eat, only licked what is her most recent favorite food – baby food. I had witnessed her drink water a couple times yesterday because her box revealed three times moisture, and I was happy about that. I cleaned it. I then decided I wanted her on my lap in 'your chair' and for about 10 minutes, this is where we were. Imagine that, <u>our</u> feral ***Ching*** <u>on my lap</u> in '<u>your chair</u>'! This is a vision that will remain with me for the rest of my life. She wanted 'down', and of course, that is where she now is. I must, however, interject yet the sweetest thing; she didn't see me run into the kitchen, which is typical, and of course the next place I usually go in the morning is into my bathroom. When I returned to your chair I saw her as I passed my bathroom, sitting on the floor at the base of my commode! She was looking for me!! She loves me!!! She is choosing to lie at the base of my commode – maybe it's the cool tile floor, but I am retaining the thought of 'her love for me'!
*Jack: Of course she loves you, but I understand where you are and how you to choose to think. Everything is as it should be, and you have done your best work with her. Remember how afraid she was when we first discovered her presence on the land – look how far she has come and this is thanks to you.*

Me: I know the end is near for her and part of me really wants to have her cremated rather than be buried here in the ground. I want her ashes with yours, and later on to be with mine, in our house.
*Jack: Do as you wish My Love. I will have her spirit alive and well with me. She will be alive and well when you join us.*

## 4:42 A.M.

Well since *Ching* has taken up residence at the base of my commode, I shall use yours. I would not disturb her choice of where to be for anything. For me, it is a comforting thought that our beautiful *Ching* is safe, in our house, in my bathroom lying on the cool tile floor. She is not alone in the *Sick Bay* building, out on the land, or in the neighbor's barn. Yes, it is comforting to know she is safe, and I so appreciate your prompting me several months ago which is actually years in her life. (Remember, one of our years equals seven of theirs.)

## SAME DAY – 11:34 A.M.
### Warm silk in my lap – Ching
*This means more than a million dollars to me. Her love is saturating my being.*

*Ching* jumped on my lap this morning and has not done this very much lately, and it was overwhelming joyful for me.

## 10 MINUTES LATER

*Ching* walked out into the laundry room, and I opened yet another can of food. She actually licked some of the clear gravy – nothing more – and she went into the dining room and jumped on another chair, yet another different place for her. She has no difficulty jumping, while walking is a bit shaky. I gladly wait on her hand and foot.

**4:58 P.M.**

What a day – dear *Ching* is very unstable on her frail legs now but still willing and able to jump on my lap for a third time. I have tempted her with food more times than I can count today, but she has absolutely no interest. She is presently under the dining room table, sleeping again. It's like her body is still doing things she has been doing for a long time now, but there is no interest in sustaining it with food. Occasionally she drinks a little water. She seems to be happy with me and on me, and this I relish. I want to absolutely do anything that pleases her, and it seems that she wants the same for me. Let me add that this beautiful creature, God's creation, has no wounds. She has lived an incredibly interesting life. She has been homeless, lived for years outside, yet always came to us when she recognized where the source of food was. She was free in spirit and physically most of her life, of her own choosing.

§

**SATURDAY, JULY 6, 2013 – 3:00 A.M.**
**I did my very best, but *Ching* would not eat at all**

I am letting go now. I am not putting her alone in the portico at night, but allowing her to be free in our house, and I want you to know I truly did my best. It is God's Will now.

**8:03 A.M.**

*Ching* just walked all the way around the outside of our house – amazing since she has had no food for three days.

**8:40 A.M.**

I had been outside with *Ching* almost one hour; Maria joined us for a few minutes and petted her. How incredibly intelligent, how incredibly smart for this beautiful cat has never been outside at our house because she always lived in *The Village* or the neighbor's barn, yet she knew instantly that the bird's water fountain had water – she went straight to it, stood on the rock beside it and drank. I steadied her weak body, but she did this. She rested a couple times on the deck while I sat on the bench, watched her and petted her. She saw a mass of birds, but I think her hearing is going and so she didn't hear them until they flew away in an explosion of wing flapping. What a wonderful morning.

Years ago, do you remember *Cleo* who was the Calico who went blind, yet walked across the street and up the hill to the neighbor's property (1,000 feet or more), and lived for another four months.

*Jack: Of course I do – fabulous memories with <u>this</u> fabulous animal.*

Me: I am so happy with myself for taking the time for *Ching*. It is as good a feeling as an abundance of money, in fact better. <u>When love is expressed two ways, there is nothing that can compare.</u> <u>That is why yours and ours were so perfect and fulfilling.</u>

*Jack: You are oh so right. You gave to me everything I needed from the first moment I laid eyes on you. Remember how breathless I was?*

Me: I just remember your sweating.

*Jack: And I remember the touch of your hand on my brow, and I knew you would have to 'get used to it'.*

Me: Today I was thinking about love that we extended to each other with great ease and joy, and remembered my childhood. I was raised in a 'conditional' love environment, and I think you were too.

*Jack: That is oh so true and something I had forgotten.*

Me: You had most definitely worked through it when we met and had learned how to love in a truly unselfish way. You had forgiven and gave of yourself without conditions to your father and mother and were at peace when they both transitioned. From time to time, I find remnants of unforgiveness of me toward my mother, who was really so hard on me. As I have mentioned before, my father was easy – yet this 'ease' somehow annoyed me. It does not now. You were easy – with your loving, and I thrived on it!

**10:47 P.M.**

Since this morning excursion for *Ching*, she wants to go out all the time now and cries. Of course this morning it was cool, tonight it was not and although we went out – we did not stay very long. She is restless, and I just know that if I allowed it, she would be outside and gone somewhere to transition. I cannot permit that on these hot days and so have asked Dr. Stried to consider Monday morning for putting her to sleep. I just don't know how many days these little guys can go without any food at all. She paces right now all over the house and certainly walks when we go outside. I can see and feel her opening up and giving absolutely all she has to give. Her heart is expanding with every step she takes, for me. I remember learning the lesson through beautiful *Brandy*, in whose memory you built **CAT HAVEN** and how she wanted us to remember her looking her best. I pull forth this memory for you that night on the corner of our hot tub where *Brandy* looked so magnificent, and it was the night before she went away. I feel that *Ching* is somewhat like me and wants to have no regrets.

§

**JULY 7, 2013 – 9:30 A.M.**
**Great news – to me**

*Rozie-Bear came to The House this morning to the back deck – his first time since his best friend, **Harpo**, transitioned 3-4 weeks ago. Before that, they would come every day together to be loved, brushed and fed. For me, it was so good to see him. I fed him his favorite chicken baby food, and he ate well. Since it's going to be 106 degrees today, I'm thankful he hurried back down the driveway toward his building. The black asphalt can be painfully hot on their little feet. I'm glad I spent extra time with him today.*

§

**JULY 8, 2013 – 6:10 A.M.**
*Ching's* last day – yet the beat goes on!

This morning our precious baby, *Ching*, was so unhappy – crying, crying, crying and would not even drink fresh water 'in our house'. However, when I went to the back door she was right with me and wanted water from the bird bath. This morning she could not stretch her precious body from the rock to the edge of the bowl to drink, and so I held her while she took in over 100 laps of water!

Approximately 7:50 A.M., Dr. Stried was here and 8 A.M. *Ching* was at rest in my arms and at peace. I have chosen to get her cremated and to bring her ashes into our house.

**8:31 A.M.**

*Ching* may very well be our very last house cat; after all, we do have a *Village* of beautiful buildings that you personally built in which to house them. I had not planned on her presence until I got your promptings so loud and clear and as I have said before, I am so glad I heard you. The last months (years in *Ching's* measurement) were very, very happy, comfortable, loving and treasured. Wonderful memories that she gave, and I gave – just like us!

**8:45 A.M.**

Here I am crying my heart out while cleaning *Ching's* space and I hear other cries. There is *Mittens* all the way from *The Village* to the back deck wanting baby food, and there on the front porch is *Oreo*, *Spike* and *Zeppo*. And so, the beat goes on!

I knew we only had a short time back in February when I brought *Ching* to our house for the last time, and I believe we both made the best of it. I know I did, and I feel she did. She had the best of lives while on earth. So many years doing what she really wanted out there – feral, but connected to us for her foods, which were always the best, and the last few months (a couple of years in her time) were super good.  We both did our best together to learn, to grow, to love and appreciate.  I know she appreciated me, and I certainly appreciated her.  Jack, I'm not choosing pain, but I'm feeling pain.  It is just there, and it hurts.  I miss her already.

**6:42 P.M.**

A difficult day – a sad day, yet I was happy knowing I did my very best and had extended myself in every way possible to make this little cat's life good.  I now find that the places in our house she selected to be, are very sacred to me.  It is difficult to clean up the floor, to move her things and close the door from the portico of our house – to empty her water bowl.  I can see clearly that she tried just about every chair, at every table, in every room.  She hid in every corner, behind everything she could, especially in the last days.  She sat at the base of both commodes and in the opening of every door, as she would watch me.  I am so glad because I see her everywhere.  She understood the first 'no' and the very few I said to her in our bedroom.  I never allow cats in the bedroom, and the first time I said 'no' to her, she moved out of the room – quite remarkable.  She was a good child to me, the best child and I love her completely now and forever more.  It is comforting to have the memories tonight, and I am looking for her everywhere as I already miss the comfort such a small animal has to offer.  I miss her without doubt, but I am glad we will be together again.

§

**JULY 9, 2013**
**The perfect house guest**

I am realizing I had more of a heart connection with *Ching* in our short time together in our house (let it never be forgotten, she was on our land for many, many years) than I did with *Callie* – who was with us much longer, and all the time in our house.  However, *Brandy* was the last time I felt this close a bond to a house cat.  Let's never forget *Harpo* and a few other unique family

108

members but in such a short time; my bonding with *Ching* was deep. Her eyes revealed so much knowing, and her behavior and understanding of what I expected was phenomenal. She never scratched or destroyed anything. Once again, a perfect house guest. This gorgeous feral cat who lived in the neighbor's barn for over 10 years had a mission – to be my comfort in our house the last few months of her life. She fulfilled this mission.

## SAME DAY – 7:43 A.M.

*Lucy* has been sitting and <u>peering into the back portico screen door</u> this morning for such a long time, and <u>I do believe she has been looking for *Ching*</u>. She had been doing this every day when *Ching* was there. I certainly learned patience through beautiful *Lucy*, for who knows what she had suffered before she came to our loving space.

§

## JULY 11, 2013
## Cleaning up – after the perfect house guest

Me: Yes My Love, *Ching* was indeed a perfect house guest. I am cleaning house today, a little bit, and sweeping floors of her fur remnants. Part of me is a tad sad because I don't like the thought of sweeping her away, but I realize she is in my heart forever and therefore my thoughts are out of line.

*Jack: Exactly. Baby, she is with me now and as happy as can be. I do believe the kitten in her lingers, and I am glad you experienced that because she was a loner, by choice, but now is again like me, and by the way, I am pleased you are having conversations with a twin sister. (I had been visiting by phone with a friend and workmate of over 40 years. Her name is Doris.) Yes, you and she have been together before and yes, you have been related. You have always been the older one and therefore, she still looks up to you as she did when you were younger. She needs your help in this lifetime, as with the others. Your loyalty to her and desire to please and clean for her (which I used to do many years ago when we both lived in Houston, Texas) is from another time. She was younger and needed your care. Now she still needs.*

Me: For the record, **Oreo**, **Spike**, **Mittens**, **Betina**, **Groucho** and **Zeppo** are extremely loyal to me, especially right now. It would appear they have learned what they needed to in this life from me as their 'Mama'. They come every single day in this 100 degree heat to the front door of our house. Yes, of course, I put out food and treats but they linger and seem to enjoy my coming and going. I certainly enjoy them. **Rozie-Bear** is not as frequent in his visits, since his best friend and brother, **Harpo**, transitioned. I trust **Harpo** is a happy cat.

*Jack: Absolutely Sweetheart, never question that. <u>It is an automatic reunion for me with our babies, because the love is so strong. It bypasses what is normal – to our level of understanding.</u> One large, happy family here, as it was on earth. There are a few who still do not trust completely, but most of them do. It is amazing the work I see you still accomplishing. <u>Do not worry about how others judge you, for they do not know as we know.</u> Baby, <u>**THEY DO NOT KNOW WHAT LOVE IS. WE KNOW OF GOD'S LOVE SWEETHEART, AND THERE IS NOTHING ON EARTH LIKE IT. YOU FORGET FROM TIME TO TIME BUT QUICKLY MAKE THE CONNECTION. I NOW LIVE IN IT, AND COULD NOT BE HAPPIER.**</u>*

As I am cleaning and gently removing **Ching's** fur, her beautiful, loving face and those loving eyes I still see, which was reward beyond expression.

At the loss of an animal, I lose my sense of direction – it <u>knocks me off my feet. MY SPIRIT IS SO INTERTWINED WITH THEIRS, AND THEY BECOME A PART OF ME. Part of me is lost when they are gone. I could tell **Ching** knew it was her mission, her job while on earth – to comfort me. Whenever she would voluntarily jump on my lap to rest, I was elated. She did this every single day she was with me in our house, until the last day when I knew also as she walked around crying out loud – very loud – that she could not do this anymore. I knew</u>

her mission was accomplished, and she was a great comfort to me in ways most people would not understand. Her little body springing on me, her little body's warmth upon me, her little body's need also to receive my loving hands on her, and my hands were indeed loving upon her precious form. Her fur was like silk, and the gratitude she revealed in my touch was comfort and reward in itself. WE WERE PARTNERS.

§

# CHAPTER 9
# 2013

# I LOVE ANIMALS SO COMPLETELY
# – ALL OF THEM

(Except snakes, sorry!)

**6th year of conversation after Jack's transition**

## ILLUMINATION

Me: I have listened to more than a fair share of ministers, and they always ask God to bless the people and the businesses, but seldom the animals!

*Jack: It is only those in high places of understanding who work with the animals. You are in a high place of understanding. You are blessed Sweetheart, your work is blessed and so are you. FEW HEARTS CAN GIVE TO THE LOWEST HEARTS OF UNDERSTANDING.*

*- Page 121, I'm Always Here, Part II*
The Continuation of Love from the Other Side

Me: <u>The understanding BY animals</u> (domestic or wild) is <u>ENHANCED when we love them 'completely'</u>. I witness this often and how they grow from the FEAR space of abandonment to the trusting space of my LOVE. It can take years – but they do grow, and reveal it in their behavior – sometimes just the night before their transition. *Lucy* did this – she 'ALLOWED me to pet her entire body just the day before she left. Quite a revelation for my awareness, and hopefully for hers.

## JULY 2013
### All creatures have their own unique beauty

**To the World I Say**

Let it never be said that any cat or creature we rescued or came to us was not perfect with a tale to tell that enhanced our life, our living and learning – but allow it to be known that some speak louder – just like me!

Never let it be said or thought for the portion of even one blink of an eye, that all the creatures who came here or were brought here were not absolutely perfect, with their own unique story of beauty and interest.

§

## WEDNESDAY, JULY 17, 2013
### *Foxy* is coming 'Home' – purring all the way

*Foxy was found as a kitten in an abandoned house Jack was remodeling. She was so dainty, so agile, so enthusiastic, so quick and with such a healthy appetite.*

This morning is was obvious our darling *Foxy* was not well at all. She is situated right now in her building, **CAT HAVEN**, comfortably on the floor with water, baby food and a new scratching box with catnip. I will not put her down today because I believe she has a little more time left for loving – not the way she has lived for all of these years (15-16, I think) climbing up her favorite oak tree onto the roof of the building; however, there is a little more loving time left for both of us, I feel. Praise God we have had rain this week – a huge storm this afternoon – and this evening I emptied just under 3 ½ inches of rain from Jack's last gift to the me, the large rain gauge he had set for me in the park on his last day on Earth. Wonderful. Now the grass will green up for the deer to eat and will help our video (that I have planned) look nice. Right now, this large expanse of land is brown – and hopefully will become green.

§

## JULY 18, 2013
## My good idea

> Hurray, hurray – I had an idea, and it worked. I opened a can of tuna for *Foxy* and gave her the entire can to lick, and lick she did. She had jumped up onto the shelf by the window and took this fluid very well. Not much sustenance but better than nothing.

§

## JULY 19, 2013
## I did right by our *Foxy*
*7:55 A.M. – 8:05 A.M. Dr. Stried just left*
*Foxy is at peace – catch her spirit*

Me: She is yours now to enjoy. I know I did right by keeping *Foxy* an extra day. She enjoyed the juice from tuna and the gravy from a small can of quality food. This morning she enjoyed a walk about inside **CAT HAVEN**, and almost an hour outside with fresh water, and my hands on her while I sat still and we waited for Dr. Stried. She purred all the time – she purred her way into heaven. There is the large oak tree by the side of **CAT HAVEN** with her name on it. It was her tree; she climbed it hundreds of times to the roof of the building. Jack, there is beauty in appreciation; there is gratitude in appreciation, and I see clearly that appreciation in me, and it is beautiful.
*Jack: In life and in time, your thinking is remarkable and indeed so deep. What a lucky guy I am to have found you yet again.*
Me: Our *Oreo-Cookie* appreciates me (*Oreo* is *Harpo*, *Groucho* and *Zeppo's* sister. The other sister, *Ebony*, transitioned a while ago), and this too is beautiful. I certainly appreciate her loyalty and dedication and how she comes every day and sits outside our house (on the rocks or the marble table); she finds shade and watches our house and appreciates me. I see this – and I'm so, so grateful.

§

## JULY 23, 2013 – 8:55 P.M.
### Precious moments, *Bitsy-Boo* – precious moments with you

Oh God Jack, the summers are so hot and unbearable. I have just completed my evening rounds of feeding and nurturing our remaining babies. They're feeling the heat too and don't have much energy – like me. *Bitsy* is feeling down from this heat and her age, and I know it because I see it and feel it too. She did not have the sparkle in her eyes tonight, but I extended mine. I tempted her with three or four favorite foods, and she ate a little from each; not much, but at least a little, and then I gave my full attention to her. I found what she wanted – my hands under her chin – and there they remained for quite some time. I got a little purr, and so I know I was successful. There are ceiling fans and a floor fan, but it is still hot. However, I have done my best.

*Amber-Belle* is a joy for she is young and runs around among the ailing. I love them all Jack and can relate to the aging ones. I give all I have to give in time and energy.

§

## JULY 24, 2013 - 8:40 A.M.
### Our *Mittens* has evolved

*Mittens, Mittens, Mittens* – the last of our kittens who comes to eat on the back deck every day. I am always elated. He ate over a jar of baby food while I brushed him. I enjoyed the time together with the hummingbirds overhead. Thank you God. I don't usually give him water because it's everywhere, but today I gave a huge bowl and he drank and drank and drank.

So interesting because for most of his life, *Mittens* has been a scaredy cat, hiding when he would see us or me and certainly not allowing himself to be petted or picked up, but now he allows me to pet, brush and do just about anything I want. Picking up is not his favorite thing, but he allows it.

§

**JULY 25, 2013 – 8:03 A.M.**
**A planned video of CAT HAVEN**

Me: Jack, is this man who is coming to make the video a good man?
*Jack: Yes Sweetie, he has compassion in is heart.*
Me: Will you be there?
*Jack: What do you think?  By the way, I like your selection of what to wear.  You know I love you in hats, and this is a good hat for you.*
Me: You are so sweet.
*Jack: No, you are the sweetness in our relationship.*

§

**JULY 26, 2013**
**I'm not ready for *Bitsy* to go**

*Bitsy* came to the house this morning – very unusual.
She wouldn't go in this evening – very unusual.
She ate very little today – very unusual.  I will just have to wait and see where she is in the morning.

§

**JULY 27, 2013 – 7:20 A.M.**

It must have been the heat because this morning after a night of rainstorms and thunder, *Bitsy* came when I called her.  Thank you God for I am not ready for *Bitsy* to go.

§

# CHAPTER 10
# 2013

# GOD IS ABSOLUTELY ALL I HAVE
## – <u>HE MUST BE</u> ALL I NEED!

**6th year of conversation after Jack's transition**

## ILLUMINATION

*Darkness cannot drive out darkness;*
*Only <u>light</u> can do that.*

*Hate cannot drive out hate;*
*Only <u>love</u> can do that.*

*- Dr. Martin Luther King, Jr.*

## JULY 27, 2013
### *Lucy's* last day was a good day
*(I learned years ago, we <u>always</u> have everything we need, to meet our needs, and I obviously have everything right now that I need. God loves it when we have to trust HIM completely. All I have is God, so HE obviously <u>must be all I need</u>.)*

<u>God IS all I have – HE must be all I need</u>!

This is a morning of desperation for me, for having lost two precious cats in two weeks and this morning a third has simply gone away; our *Lucy* is not here. Yesterday I wrote about a lesson I learned from *Lucy*, and it is a great lesson, but I now need her to truly bond with. We had a good day yesterday, for she actually 'allowed' me to seriously pet her head and back and seemed to enjoy it. Let it be understood *Lucy* always wanted to be seen, but never allowed touch; she seemed to enjoy people – but not other cats. Yesterday, I believe it her jealousy of *Rozie-Bear* to whom I was also giving special attention because I could see that he too is aging fast. However, we finally had the bond, and for the rest of the day, *Lucy* appeared to be happy, using all the lovely resting spaces provided for her on the back decks and front porch, and yet <u>this morning</u>, she is not here. I know she is not sick, but is she hurt?

*Jack: No. This is a test for you. Let go, let God take over Sweetheart. This is what you must do for us.*

And the beauty of it is – IF *Lucy* <u>has really gone, and you tell me she is not hurt, it is 'her choice'</u> – and <u>her last day with me, was a good day</u>. She was loved by and assured of my love and seemed to respond to my love by 'allowing' it. I was happy with her; I was proud of her and told her so. She had spent the early evening on her table, on her soft cool cushion scratching with all fours on her new cardboard corrugated scratching board, and I was happy. She was happy but now she is gone! Once again, I realize <u>her last day was a good day</u>, and <u>everything is as it should be, you say</u>.

§

## SAME DAY – 1:30 P.M.

I saw your butterfly spirit briefly when Maria was leaving today. Thank you, you have no idea how comforting that is.

## SAME DAY, JULY 27 – <u>8:25 P.M.</u>
### *Rozie-Bear's* last night

Me: *Rozie-Bear* was gasping for air in the long outside run of his building (the *Ruffhouse)* this evening; will he make it through the night?
*Jack: He is not well right now and ready to come home.*

## LATER THAT NIGHT – <u>10:05 P.M.</u>

Well, <u>*Rozie* has transitioned!</u>  I received your prompting and went down with a flashlight to check on him.  He was not in the <u>outside run area</u> where I left him just a few hours earlier, so I was pleased that he was <u>inside</u> his building.  I didn't see him until I checked underneath the water platform.  He was already stretched out and cold.  I promptly and gently pulled him out, got him in his bed on blue satin, and he is now lying in his building with his friends.  It is a relief for me in that I don't have to bother Dr. Stried to come and put him to sleep.  *Rozie* went in his 'own timing'.  Everything is exactly as it should be, you say – certainly not the way I want it but as God wants it.  I am tired, very tired, emotionally and physically.  Please be with me tonight.

## JULY 27, 2013
### Summary of *Rozie's* last day
*Rozie-Bear*, beautiful in size and personality – FOREVER loyal

Good, very good.  He walked all the way to the house (400 ft. one way) to the back deck and ate 2/3 of a jar of baby food.  He would have eaten more, but I said 'no' because I wanted the remaining third for *Mittens*.  He drank water from a special bowl I keep for him inside the back fountain, because he seems to enjoy drinking here.  He spent the morning sleeping by the bird's water pan at

*The Wellhouse*, in the shade. I carried him in my arms ½ the way down to his house, and Maria carried him the rest of the way and put him inside his building. All in all – a good morning.

## LATER
*I would suppose I was feeling sad because so many of our babies had made their transition and I said:*

Me: Well, I'm going to feed what is left of our babies, that is those who are still here.

**Jack: THEY ARE ALL HERE SWEETHEART, JUST ON A DIFFERENT VIBRATION.**

§

## JULY 28, 2013 – 7:22 A.M.
## My love opened *Lucy's* heart – Maria opened *Happy's*

*Jack tells me **Lucy** is in heaven today – a much happier and more friendly spirit than she was on the earth plane.*

**Jack: Your love opened her heart.**
Me: Wow, that's what love does – it makes us even <u>more</u> loving. I had certainly done my best where *Lucy* was concerned, loving her day after day, year after year and <u>on her last day</u>, she 'accepted it'. Is that how it is with us on our last day, we accept God's love? Let it be known that <u>I accept His love NOW</u>, long before my last day. No, no, no God – <u>I ACCEPT YOU this holy instant</u>. Thank you, praise you for loving me day after day, year after year; <u>you have been there in love subliminally and like **Lucy**, not every day have I been with an open heart to receive it. Let it not escape me ever again. GOD, I KNOW HOW YOU MUST FEEL WHEN WE ACCEPT YOUR LOVE, BECAUSE I KNOW HOW I FELT WHEN **Lucy** FINALLY ACCEPTED MINE.</u> No more *Lucy-Goosey* (I named her this because she was ever resistant to touch and blessings.) <u>She is my beloved **Lucy** now</u> and her nameplate is permanently placed outside our house because this is where she claimed 'home', and this is where

she finally surrendered to my love – God's love.

 I spent a few minutes thinking about some of the cats who have transitioned since Jack's departure and *Happy* came to mind. Why we ever called him *Happy*, I cannot recall, other than he was perhaps a happier kitten, but in his last days he was seemingly unfriendly toward me. He just wanted the food. I was remembering that most of our cats were <u>very</u> happy, and I knew their hearts were open at their time to move on, but *Happy* I was not sure about. I said to Jack, "I don't know if I opened his heart."
*Jack: If you didn't, then Marie did, for he was ready, and he is happy here.*

### 9:37 A.M.
### *Betina* was a little love goddess today

*Betina*, who was found in a drainage ditch about 13 years ago in Round Rock, Texas – is a <u>very</u> loving cat and has the silkiest fur coat of any cat we have had. She lives in *Pardy's* pen and her two remaining friends are *Oreo* and *Sooty*. She has been coming to *The House* in the mornings for baby food, and this morning I allowed her to come <u>into</u> *The House*. She was loud at first in her cries, and then silence. She found the chair with our copy of *"The Prophet"* Kahlil Gibran's book opened to "LOVE", and surrounding it were 'our books'. She is sleeping on them all right now – a beautiful sight, and certainly good for my heart.

### 10:18 A.M.
### A 'first' – for me

An example of how "few hearts can give to the lowest hearts of understanding":
We had rain last night – about ¾ of an inch. I have noticed before when the back deck gets wet, dozens of snails appear. Well, *Mittens* had his usual baby food this morning and left traces of it on the paper plate from which he was eating – and the snails found it. Some of the snails are no bigger than a 1/8 to a ¼ of an inch in diameter. I retrieved the plate and smeared more baby

food all over it and guess what, the snails are already crawling to and eating that food. Yes, the snails are eating the baby food. Too funny for words! (The lowest hearts of understanding, I would say!)

**10:37 A.M.**

I checked, and the snails had cleaned the plate and were gone. I placed the plate on a marble table, not on the ground, and the snails were crawling away on the other side of the table, pretty fast. I guess they were reenergized.

§

## MONDAY, JULY 29, 2013
**– In the wee small hours of the morning**
**The soul's knowing is so deep**

Me: I am finding that the British comedies and movies I see on TV are very well written and portrayed, and seeing England as they depict I am happy to reunite in my mind, with my heritage. I have just watched almost two hours of totally fascinating stuff. Now it is time for bed, but I'm not too tired so here I am thinking about the events of the past two weeks. Yes, two weeks ago *Ching* was here and so was *Foxy*.

*Jack: Baby, <u>they are still with you no matter how you think</u>. They love you and will never leave you, but I am enjoying their spirits with bated breath. They are both indeed beautiful – as are you. I know where you're thoughts have been today* (let it be known my thoughts have been into this, our third book, *Everlasting Love – That is*) *and <u>I know how amazed I am at your astute thinking of me and my actions as a young man</u>. <u>You are bringing to my own realization what occurred for me – without my knowing at that time – what was happening for me</u>. <u>Yes, you see clearly now what I did not, in those early years of my life</u>* (when Jack was 22 years of age). *<u>And yes, God did have me in His palm and yes, My Love, I was in Vietnam – scared to death, yet knowing all was well</u>. <u>THE SOUL'S</u>*

## KNOWING IS SO DEEP, SO UNREVEALED – UNTIL SO MUCH LATER.

§

**JULY 29, 2013 – 8:19 A.M.**
**Jack really knows what's going on!**

> I was thinking that Maria was late because although I had been checking through the window from *The House*, she was not yet here and her starting time is 8:00 A.M. I said out loud, "I just know she is here right now," as I walked to the door to check yet again. I heard Jack say, ***"Yes, she is here, she is bringing in the garbage cans."*** I didn't think much about it until I checked and there she was – bringing in the garbage cans!

§

**TUESDAY, JULY 30, 2013**
**Our *Bitsy's* eyes – say so much**
Me: For the record, this evening was one of the best ever with our *Bitsy* and *Amber-Belle*. Bitsy had me worried several days ago when she would not allow me to pick her up and put her inside the **CAT HAVEN** building for the night. There are many, many places for cats to sleep safely outside, but *Bitsy* is getting frail and I wanted her to be safe. I allowed her to be happy, to be outside, and there was a strong thunderstorm that night. The next morning I called her, and she came running from the space we created behind the *Cat House* and ran into her home inside the **CAT HAVEN** building. She has been inside the **CAT HAVEN** building for several days now and although looking a little more frail, tonight she ate well and allowed me to pet, brush, comb and love her. She actually drank cat milk for the first time and ate catnip. I was happy, she was happy and all is well this memorable evening. Thank you God for the good memories. By the way, *Belle* was part of this entire evening experience and received special attention from me.
*Jack: Good job Babe, good job. Yes, our Bitsy has come a long way*

*for sure. You will remember the first time she ever allowed me just to pet her and how overwhelmed with emotion I was.*

Me: I remember so well your tears – I thought something bad had happened but not so – *Bitsy* had allowed you to touch her. She does not like to be picked up, but she does like to be petted and scratched. She has incredible eyes – they say so much.

§

**JULY 31, 2013 – 8:55 A.M.**
**My rewards**

Thrill upon thrill for me this morning – no one else but me. *Mittens* is here on the back deck eating his baby food. He is very easy to please – just give him canned food. *Oreo* is always the first to the front of the house, she's not quite so easy – no longer likes baby food, but prefers something else –and everyday it seems to be different. Because she didn't eat the baby food and *Zeppo* does, I called him (*Zeppo, Zeppo, Zeppo*). He's usually here but this morning not so. I went into our house for a minute or two, and then looked outside and to my sweet surprise, *Groucho* was there. He probably had not been to our house since your transition (six years now), so this was joyous for me. *Zeppo* is his brother and I guess at a distance, the names sound alike. I was weeping with joy to see him. He's very thin now and certainly not the enormous cat he was, but obviously he is alert. He did not like the baby food but certainly enjoyed the canned salmon that was on the plate.

**LATER THAT A.M.**
*Linen* (one of the five kittens who came here four years ago after Jack's transition)

**A.M.** *Linen* was here and ate well.

**P.M.** No *Linen*

§

127

**AUGUST 1, 2013**
**A.M.** No *Linen*

**P.M.** – No *Linen*

> What's going on? He's one of the youngest cats here, and he's gone. 106 degree heat may have something to do with it, but I simply don't know. I certainly want him to come home.

§

**FRIDAY, AUGUST 2, 2013**
**A.M.** No *Linen*, **but the reward today is** *Mittens*
Me: Still no *Linen* but the reward is *Mittens*, who is on the <u>kitchen window sill</u>. A reward for me because he has never been there. I went out to check on and to pet him and oh dear, he is not well, but he is doing his best – for me, I know. I feel he is getting as close to me as he can and showing love, and it is returned – you know that.
*Jack: <u>Baby, I know, and they know. I am with you and see it all. This is the process; do not deplete yourself when you know this is how it's supposed to be. It's how God planned it. Keep doing and keep learning for this is the perfection of your soul for eternity. You are on course and timing is perfect</u>.*

**P.M.** No *Linen*

§

**SATURDAY, AUGUST 3, 2013**
**A.M.** *Linen* **is back**

> *LINEN* IS HERE. Three days gone, and he behaves like nothing's happened! I embraced him with such gratitude that he recognized my voice and made the journey to see me.

§

## SUNDAY, AUGUST 4, 2013 – 8:33 A.M.
### God's power revealed through His creatures

The hummingbirds, this very minute, are enjoying the fresh syrup I put out last night. So few people know how good it feels to witness this unless they truly love the creatures.

Bonus – *Mittens* is here on the back deck drinking the fresh water I placed for him. Now he is eating the baby food and other canned food he likes. I am filled with joy to see him, yet another day, thank you God. There is sweet *Oreo*, who is *Harpo's* sister eating the other half jar of baby food. The effort these cats put forth to be at *The House* where I am is astounding. It is their love that I witness. God's power is revealed through his creatures – I see this – which is my payment for the day.

Dozens of birds are filling the feed tables – this is without question my favorite time of the day. I think this is the most beautiful place in the whole world – every time I look outside, there is something wonderful going on. Deer all over the hillside, squirrels in and out of the dog houses you built – René saw rabbits here this morning – they were plentiful when we first moved here, but their presence has dwindled as the years have passed. I love what I do and where I do it!

**LATER**

Me: Jack, I know you know I know I have everything I need. Not necessarily everything I want, but everything I need.

*Jack: You will have everything you want Sweetheart. It is written in the stars.*

§

## AUGUST 6, 2013
### Video Day

*Betina* - a movie star today! (Totally black, 'silky', short-haired female about 13 years old. She was found in a drainage ditch in Round Rock, Texas.) Author video being shot today, and *Betina* was queen for a day! (See her on YouTube - http://youtu.be/R4_S687shJ4)

§

129

**AUGUST 15, 2013 – 7:25 A.M.**

**Confirmation that I am doing what I am supposed to be doing**

*I was missing **Lucy** due to her recent transition, and thinking I perhaps had not been patient enough or done enough for her.*

*Jack: Sweetheart, stop punishing yourself; it is not necessary.* <u>***BELIEVE IT OR NOT, BUT ANIMALS HAVE LESSONS TO LEARN TOO.***</u> *She saw love, and finally learned to accept love and* <u>*proved this on her last day 'to you', if not before 'for her'.*</u> *You gave her what she needed and certainly what she wanted. You gave your all. Have no regrets for she is here now and although she keeps somewhat to herself, her light reveals the truth of what she learned.*
Me: Thank you. <u>I would never be who and how I am today if it were not for you Jack.</u>
*Jack:* <u>***YOU AND YOUR GROWTH ALLOW ME TO FLY HIGHER.***</u>
*Yes,* <u>***WHAT YOU DO WHERE YOU ARE AFFECTS WHAT I DO WHERE I AM.***</u>

**LATER**
Me: The man I met today, a Scotsman, outside PetSmart who admired my simple gesture of putting food for the birds – I told him it was what I did – I had a refuge for animals and at that moment while I was speaking, I received a message from Spirit to give him a book (our first book, *Listen, I'm Still Here*) and a card indicating a link to our second book (*I'm Always Here*); I felt the need to help him. He was really down and had even quit a good job as a result of death in his family. I felt that he was another indication that what I am doing in my life is the right thing for me to be doing – which is helping animals. He was reassuring me from God that what I am doing is right, for me. Am I right?
*Jack: Yes My Love. He does need help, and you and I should extend that whenever the opportunity presents itself, and yes you are most definitely doing the right thing, and yes there is another quality man who will be a companion and helpmate to you.*
Me: Bring me a man whose hand I can hold, to bring me the warmth of you.
*Jack: That is certainly something I promise to do.*

§

# CHAPTER 11
# 2013

# I KNOW HOW GOD MUST FEEL
## – WHEN WE TURN TO AND TRUST HIM COMPLETELY

### 6th year of conversation after Jack's transition

## ILLUMINATION

*Time alone with God
is the answer to all things.*

## AUGUST 2013
### Learning to accept God's Love

*Jack explains things to me and I think what I am now understanding is that before we accept God's love, because we are all entitled, but not always do we allow or accept it. And this is what I am learning through my animals – they are all entitled for they all certainly have it, but not always do they allow or accept it. It is in their acceptance of our love that I recognize how God must feel when we accept His.*

### To the World I Say

GOD LOVES IT WHEN WE HAVE TO DEPEND ON HIM – I DO. WE HAVE TO LEARN TO DEPEND ON THE INVISIBLE. I have learned through the growth of the animals that my life is wrapped around, and I see this growth so clearly through them. 10 years of a cat's life equals 70 years of ours. This is about how long it takes most of us to come to this level of understanding, 'the meaning of life'.

When 'our' cats, who for 10 years or more, still reject the loving care we have always extended to them and suddenly recognize and appreciate the safety and turn their fears to acceptance of our love, I know exactly how God must feel when after 70 years or more we recognize and accept the safety of 'His' love and presence, and let go of our fears and allow and accept the love He extends to us. WE MUST ACCEPT THE MIRACLE!

§

## AUGUST 16, 2013 – 7:25 A.M.
### Highest and deepest love

Me: **ONLY TODAY, SIX MONTHS AFTER YOU TOLD ME,** *"We have the highest and deepest love that two souls can bathe in."* **DO I KNOW WHAT KIND OF LOVE THAT IS – GOD'S LOVE. WE HAVE THAT, WE RECOGNIZE AND ACCEPT IT - AND NOT EVERYBODY DOES. ACCEPT IT, THAT IS. WE ARE BLESSED BEYOND MEASURE.**
*Jack: Yes, Baby, we are.*

Me: A remarkable day today – a day of extraordinary growth and understanding. A day of understanding God's love and believe it or not, I think our *Oreo* (a long-haired black and white female cat, sister to *Harpo*, *Groucho*, *Zeppo* and *Ebony*) is part of my understanding. *Oreo*, and *Spike* (a short-haired black male, a friend of hers from another building) are my biggest fans. *Oreo* is quite a kitty! She has taken *Lucy* and *Ching's* place at our house. She is as close to *The House* always and therefore, as close to me as she can get. She is joy for me, and I am grateful for this showing of love. She will not come into the house, although I have invited by opening the door many times, yet she lies at the door opening every day. I am blessed. This is charming and revealing of her love. TO GAIN THE TRUST OF AN ABANDONED ANIMAL IS SO SPECIAL, AND I KNOW EXACTLY HOW GOD FEELS WHEN WE TRUST HIM. HE IS GRATEFUL AS I AM GRATEFUL. AND YES, I KNOW HOW GOD FEELS.

§

**SUNDAY, AUGUST 18, 2013 – 9:52 A.M.**
**The birds are watching me**

Yes Jack, the birds are watching me, and it is a wonderful feeling. Marie had placed the daily bowls of food for the birds on the triangular tables at the back of our house about an hour ago and for some reason this afternoon, I felt the need to put more food today. There was a magnificent couple – a male and a female I presumed (variety unknown but very colorful) hopping around an almost empty table because between the birds and the squirrels, they had 'licked the platter clean'. My heart opened and so did the food barrel and I put another half bowl on each table yet again. Before I arrived back in the kitchen – and you know that was a minute – the tables were covered with birds!! I was thrilled at this sight.

Hummingbirds are another story. It has been so hot, and I have kept the syrup fresh; yet, I don't see many birds. I will keep the syrup out until the end of October, but perhaps some have gone further south for the winter already. I don't know. Early departures, I have observed it happen in other years.

**LATER**

Me: I am so grateful God to know what it is like to be loved, even when you know you are not perfect.

*Jack: But to me and to God, you were and still are, beyond description.*

§

**AUGUST 25, 2013**

**Everybody is looking for what we have**

Me: Everybody is looking for what we have Jack – *Everlasting, "Love"- That Is.* Everybody, absolutely everybody wants what we have.

*Jack: EVENTUALLY THEY WILL HAVE IT, BUT MOST WILL LIVE MANY LIFETIMES, AS WE DID, TO ACHIEVE THIS.*

**LATER**

**Your greatest gift to me – by your example and gentle teachings**

Me: You re-introduced me to God. Your acceptance of me just the way I was, with all of my nonsense. You seemed to enjoy it – allowing me to be me, that is.

*Jack: Oh Sweetheart, I did. I saw your compassion, your loving attentiveness to everything you were involved with; your attention to detail and perfection in completion of tasks for us, for our business and for yourself.*

**SAME DAY**

**Beautiful sights**

Me: *Sooty* and *Linen* – brothers – kittens who came to us three years ago through their mother I named *Zipper* and their father I named *Frenly,* found each other today in a loving way and sat together on a marble table at the back of our house. (They obviously recognized they were related.) René took their picture; a beautiful sight for me.

*Jack: Beautiful for them too My Love, just beautiful.*

## SAME DAY

> How loving the deer are. Our back hillside is covered with deer right now, searching the ground for something 'alive' to eat. And because we are in a drought and I know there is no grass, I realized they are probably already searching for acorns – I must presume have fallen – but deer <u>know</u> it is becoming that special time of the year yet again for this source of food.

§

## AUGUST 26, 2013 – SIX MINUTES AFTER MIDNIGHT
### Acknowledgement of beautiful sights

Me: God, in a recap of yesterday's visions – <u>I thank you for the reunion of these two brothers; maybe a reunion of 'just cats', but symbolic of the reunion of brothers. By your Grace, this comes about for all of us. I live in YOUR POWER and rest in YOUR LOVE and Divine guidance with deep appreciation for all your goodness.</u>
*Jack: <u>You are such a good girl, and I RELISH IN THE GROWTH OF YOUR SWEET SOUL TO WHERE I FLY AND BASK IN ITS TRANSFORMATION. I see this Sweetheart; I see every step you take.</u>*

§

## AUGUST 26, 2013 – 12:29 A.M.
### Every cell of my DNA feels love

> I think my writings will end when I meet my new gentleman friend who thinks like me and who will enjoy my company, and that will be nice.

*But for now, I live in a state of overwhelm – God's Love. Every cell of my DNA feels love.*

## LATER THAT MORNING – 5:54 A.M.
**An early morning thought**

God, I love you so much. I appreciate all you have done for and given to me. Of course, my Jack is the most precious gift for the peace of my mind and the growth of my soul, a perfect partner and husband for me and a perfect son for you. I find no fault in him. Harmonious blending God, the Great One – the Perfect Love. WE HAVE IT – MY JACK AND I! WE ACCEPT IT! YOUR LOVE!

§

## AUGUST 29, 2013 – 10:33 A.M.
**Butterfly reflection – Jack had my back**

Jack, I know you are here – I saw your butterfly reflection as I walked down the driveway. It was refreshing in the heat of the mid-day sun to witness the shadow reflection of a huge butterfly over my head as I walked down the driveway with both of my hands full of papers and garbage! It was wonderful to see and know you had my back!

§

## SEPTEMBER 6, 2013 – 10:20 P.M.
**A video for posterity – of CAT HAVEN**

Me: You know exactly what took place today on our magnificent land. Yes, a very gracious gentleman (Brad, who was the professional filmmaker for our book promotion video, returned today to do something personal for us). He was here for a second time, filming our land and how it should look – for future caretakers to note. It has been a lot of hard work getting this space, the buildings and the land, to look the way we like it so that the expectation we have of the maintenance of our creation is now on film. I wanted this, and I believe you have supported my decision.

*Jack: Without doubt Sweetheart. It has been a prompting of mine for some time. The young man you have spent time with is good in*

137

*many ways, and his creation will be exactly what you have wanted. I am more than glad you have accomplished this.*

Me: You know I had told him I did not want to be seen, and I did not want to be heard.  This video is not about me but only about our creation and how it should look.  At one point, I asked you if you were going to reveal your presence yet again, and I believe you said, *"Like you, I don't need to be seen."*  Was I correct?

Jack: Exactly.  **I WAS THERE FOR THE WORLD TO SEE IN THE PROMOTING OF OUR BOOK** (which had occurred several weeks before with the video promotion for our second book, *I'm Always Here*, Part II and is shown on YouTube – Dorothy Farley, *I'm Always Here*).

§

## SEPTEMBER 7, 2013
### I continue pride in our *Mittens*

I am so proud of *Mittens*.  *Mittens* was always so fearful you know, difficult to get into his building, difficult in so many ways, didn't want to be picked up and always a super scaredy-cat and yet now, almost at the end of his life, he is so sweet, loves to be petted, runs to the house every morning for food and cat milk.  He comes when I call him, loves to be brushed and has very little fear.  It is wonderful to see this growth.

§

**SEPTEMBER 2013**
**Small miracles at CAT HAVEN**
Following is a list of champion kitties at **CAT HAVEN** who have come SO far from FEAR to TRUST to LOVE:

### Remaining Champion Kitties who now
### know love and how to give and receive it

- *Amber-Belle*
- *Bitsy*
- *Betina*
- *Crystal*
- *Frenly*
- *Groucho*
- *Joy*
- *Linen*
- *Lynn*
- *Maudie*
- *Mittens*
- *Neecy*
- *Opal*
- *Oreo*
- *Rose*
- *Sooty*
- *Spike*
- *Spotty*
- *Zeppo*

- Our *Spike* is very loyal to me and his house companion, *Mittens*; he comes to the front door everyday – maybe for treats, but nevertheless he allows me to pet him.

- *Oreo* (*Harpo's* sister) is here every day also. She is very thin now, and it is not from lack of food for she eats plenty. She accepts hand petting and love. She's very beautiful and seems to understand what I say. When the driveway is so hot from the sun, she sits in the shade, and I take baby food <u>to her</u>. She has been loyal for many years now. When the cats come to where I am and watch for me daily, I know we have a good thing going. For me, it is absolutely 'money in the bank' – that feeling of enrichment. Just outside the door right this minute, *Oreo* is resting on my old, stinky, filthy work shoes! Just outside the door, what grand love this expresses. I am loved by *Oreo*; her face is in the heel of my smelly shoe!! Thank you God, I have eyes that see, and a heart open to your wonders.

- *Zeppo (Harpo's* brother) is also finding his way to *The House* of late, and to me. He is more allowing than he ever used to be, either through his own growth or from watching others.

Most of the animals who do come to *The House* can see this building from where they live in *The Village* of cat buildings and therefore, they can see me come and go. Some of their buildings are not within sight of our house and therefore, they don't actually visit, but my reception is the same when I am within their sight.

When, in what I now know to be their last days with me and they allow me to kiss their head, I know the bond is there, the love is there, forever more. There is peace for me, and I'm happy. I so love my animals. My Mission with and for them is complete.

Thank you God that we will all be together again. I could not bear to think of it any other way. For me and my personal level of understanding, it is the only way to think.

§

# CHAPTER 12
## 2013

# I HAVE ENOUGH TIME
## – DIVINE TIMING PREVAILS

### 6th year of conversation after Jack's transition

## ILLUMINATION

*Anything which is good in me*
*is the effect of God's mercy – that and nothing else.*

*-- St. Therese*

§

*Commit your work to the Lord,*
*and your plans will be established.*

*-- Proverbs 16:3*

## SEPTEMBER 8, 2013 – 10:45 A.M.
## I have enough time – Divine Timing prevails

Me: Hopefully, as of this date, I have finally mastered a huge lesson – for me. I now know in my heart that <u>I have enough time to do all that I need to do on this Earth plane to satisfy my soul's yearning for completion of earthly tasks</u>.

Jack, I feel as of this date that although so many things for me and for the Trust are not yet complete, I have enough time to do that. So many legal documents need to be revised or completed. So many people are needed to replace me and learn all that I do here for our charitable trust. So much unfinished business, and yet I no longer have the fear I have had for so many years. I am in the wonderful space of <u>knowing God has it all under control</u>. I am just doing what I feel I am able to do each day without stress but only enjoyment, appreciation and sweet memories of 'us'. These memories keep the light around me and my spirit flying high. Everything is in Divine Order. Divine timing prevails. God has <u>me</u> in the palm of His hand, and I am so grateful at the loss of the fear of not doing enough.

*Jack: Oh Sweetheart, that is the best news ever for me. You are so right, God has you exactly where He wants you. He knows of your trust and is blessed with your faith. To fulfill your wishes is His joy and certainly mine. You will be amazed at what the future holds in store for you. Your effort, your work – our work – will receive just rewards. My pride overwhelms me.*

Me: Yes, for someone who was always told growing up that 'you cannot do this or that', I have broken the barrier of my doubt. And yes, I now know what I am capable of with the trust you taught me and the encouragement you have always directed toward me. You too have been my help in every need. I cannot image a heart being more grateful than mine.

§

**SEPTEMBER 9, 2013 – 8:59 P.M.**
**I so miss the romance of you**

Me: I have just finished watching a thoroughly charming and romantic movie – so sweet and so pure in its message, and it reminded me of the romance of you. You never, ever missed a chance to do and say or behave in the most romantic, charming, sweet and wonderful manner. You were an absolute champion where romance was concerned. I wonder who taught you because I don't believe it was <u>your father</u>.

*Jack: That's for sure. No my love, <u>it was my heart's desire to please you in all and any ways that I could. I knew the sweetness and purity of you and wanted to justify my behavior to honor you.</u> Again, <u>it is the soul's longing and growth to please where we know it will be appreciated.</u> You always acknowledged my behavior in some way, and I knew of your gratitude. I certainly know now!*

Me: I say what an incredible man.

*Jack: I say what a phenomenal woman.*

Me: <u>To know this level of consumable love exists should be known to the world</u>.

*Jack: <u>It is only through God's love that it is possible. We have it – and it is available to everyone who makes the choice to accept it.</u> We made the choice.*

Me: You were the teacher; for without your teaching, I doubt I would have known.

*Jack: You are now the teacher, so make it known to others. This is the message – our message. <u>WE ARE ALL ONE WITH GOD AND HIS LOVE. The message is for everyone, everywhere.</u> We have the "Everlasting, "Love" That Is", and no one can take that from us. We claim it and have for lifetimes. <u>You had forgotten and disconnected when I came back into your life and helped you to reclaim and again, hookup to what has always been yours. THAT WAS MY PURPOSE WITH YOU, TO HELP YOU RECONNECT TO GOD AND HIS POWER.</u> Your life experiences this time around had <u>allowed you to disconnect, but my love and God's love showed you the way back. NOW YOU KNOW IT IS YOURS FOR ETERNITY – THAT IS</u>.*

Me: The simplicity has me in overwhelm.

*Jack: I know.*

Me: You were so large and masculine in stature, yet you knew just how sensitive and feminine you needed to be to relate to miniature me. However, you had mastered this and were my 'masterful companion'. God had you in the palm of His hand in your relationship to me. You made no wrong moves. I was overwhelmed and didn't always respond to you as I would now. I HAD SO MUCH LEARNING TO PERFECT FOR YOU.

*Jack: Not at all.  I HAD MUCH TO LEARN TO BE AS YOU WANTED.  I know now my feelings and wish too that I could have been better.  Like you, I did my best but would do better next time! Learning never ceases.*

*Reference I'm Always Here, Part II, Page 68*

Me: Some who have read our book frequently ask me about your work.

*Jack: It is of no importance to anyone but God, and you may tell them so.*

Me: I will.

*Jack: It is not important what we do over here, it is only important what you do there. Keep growing!*

§

## SEPTEMBER 11, 2013
## Learning to accept what is

Me: Jack, God has me in a very strange place. I have absolutely nothing I once had with you. I don't have you; I don't have the fun we had; I don't have anything I once had with you and enjoyed so much. I don't have friends who think like me; I've been buying things I will never use and don't need. If you had been here, I would have used them and needed them. Yes, I love the animals and doing for them; and yes, I love the land and working on it. I enjoy writing very much, but it has not as yet given me any rewards. I don't have any rewards for my work. When will this change and fulfill me?

*Jack: AS SOON AS YOU LET GO OF WHAT WAS, AND ACCEPT WHAT IS.*

Me: Life with you was so much pleasure, so much fun, so much enjoyment, and so much love. What you brought to my life made my life perfectly wonderful. Now there is only me. Not one friend in the flesh, not one to talk to – and I'm not happy about that. Not one who thinks like me. All work and no play is making me a very dull girl.

*Jack: You will never be dull – your nature is full of life and fun.*

Me: Then why don't I have anyone to share with?

*Jack: Timing Baby, God's timing.*

Me: Well, right now He needs to know I'm not fulfilled!!

*Jack: He already knows that.*

Me: I guess I just have to break some bad habits that I thought were okay because with you, they were. They had purpose and fulfillment and lots of enjoyment. My mind is full, and I mean full of what needs to be done here, what is breaking down (including me) and what needs to be repaired and replaced. It is work, work, work in my mind and body, and I have absolutely no support. Why is that? What am I doing wrong?

*Jack: Nothing except storing fear that is not necessary.*

Me: I would like to <u>visually see</u> I can accomplish my tasks instead of just '<u>knowing</u>'.

*Jack: But that is not how it works. <u>IT IS THE KNOWING THAT GOD WILL NOT LET YOU DOWN THAT THE STRENGTH COMES</u>.*

Me: I have days like that, but it is difficult while in the flesh to maintain it.

*Jack: But that is what needs to be. Trust, trust, trust – I tell you about this often. <u>BABY, YOU ARE A CHOSEN ONE. WE ARE A CHOSEN COUPLE. DO YOU THINK YOU WILL BE FORGOTTEN, NEGLECTED?</u>*

Me: Sometimes I guess I do.

*Jack: Then stop.*

Me: My life with you was so much fun, so much pleasure, just so much of everything good. I am a spoiled brat!

*Jack: Not so. Don't be so hard on yourself. Just get yourself out of the way and do the good work. All is well – I promise, and I guarantee it.*

**LATER – 9:25 P.M.**

Me: I'm sorry God, so sorry, but this man you have given me was such a perfect partner, perfect husband, perfect friend, perfect companion, perfect comforter – just plain perfect. I would suppose as a result, I am spoiled. There will never be another companion like him, but to have someone who <u>thinks</u> like me and <u>enjoy my company would be nice</u>.

**GOD: He is there My Child, perfect for you at this time. He too has work to do to be ready for you. It is all arranged. You have been friends in another life, so the comfort will be immediate. Your Jack knows of this, and is happy too.**

Me: <u>I don't want to let you go Jack.</u>

*Jack: **Baby, you don't have to. I am always, always with you wherever you go and whoever you are with – there is no separation. You can have everything, and me included. You can have it all, and I will share it with you. WE ARE ALL ONE MY LOVE. You and I and God and your friends are all ONE – no separation. EVERYTHING IS GOD, and I never leave your side.***

Me: You know how I am turned inside out with love for you.

*Jack: **Yes I do Sweetie, and it is returned. It is only your mind that cannot believe – your soul knows it all, past, present and future which is all right now. YOU HAVE IT ALL RIGHT NOW – YOUR DREAMS ARE ALL FULFILLED RIGHT NOW. They are my dreams too.***

Me: You are so right. I cannot believe I am deserving of someone as good as you. I am a very grateful girl, very grateful.

§

**SEPTEMBER 12, 2013**
**Relishing in the pleasure of you**

Me: Michele could not come to work on our Book III today, so I am cleaning out a closet – the closet in <u>your</u> room where I had stored in <u>your</u> huge suitcase our special trinkets and memories that for some reason I had wanted right after your transition, to hide or secure. I will never know why I did what I did, but anyhow, I am so happy today to have the opportunity to renew the memories of us, of you and the very first astrological comparisons that were prepared by Datha Fowler (an incredibly gifted astrologer), for us. You and I were definitely directed to each other and there is no doubt about that now. The gifts we brought to each other and the lessons we learned from each other are quite astonishing. Yes, this morning I am relishing in the pleasure of you on yet another level of understanding.

You know, this morning there are so many crows squawking here (or ravens, I am told), and so I have just put out a second bowl of seeds, hoping to shut them up. Fortunately, there is a large selection of choice seeds and nuts in the barrels and within two minutes there was a mass of tiny birds enjoying this feast. This sight always makes my life feel worthwhile.

*Jack: Oh boy, your life is most certainly worthwhile. Never doubt that.*

**LATER**
1:20 P.M.

Me: I think I saw your butterfly shadow as I was walking down the driveway to close the gate a few minutes ago.

*Jack: You definitely did. You are in rare form today – very attentive to me and to God, and I like that a lot.*

Me: That is exactly what you would say when you were here in physical form.

*Jack: It is no different where I am now. I like your attention on me – and on God!*

§

**SEPTEMBER 13, 2013**
**We live on hallowed ground**

Me: Jack, you know we have always thought this land was an old Indian burial ground with the thousands of little flint rocks visible so high up and away from the creek bed, and today, A.D. Pitcher confirmed that this is his thinking also. (Mr. Pitcher is a gentleman whose creative work is displayed here in our awnings.)

*Jack: Yes Sweetie, it is. <u>Now I know for sure it is hallowed ground we live on</u>.*

§

## SEPTEMBER 14, 2013
## WE ARE ALL ONE

Me: Do you remember the first time you saw me?

*Jack: Oh boy, do I.*

Me: And I remember the first time I saw you – my bearded wonder unraveling yourself from the hotel chair. I was in shock you were so powerfully handsome to me.

*Jack: And you were so beautifully beautiful to me!*

Me: It was love at first breath of sight, wasn't it?

*Jack: Absolutely. So many lifetimes remembered in that first second, but Baby, <u>you cannot live in the past when there is so much that is beautiful coming up for you</u>.*

Me: I want to, I want to. I cannot imagine anything more beautiful than what was.

*Jack: But Sweetheart, I'm going to be with you through the new – trust me. I will be there for all of it.*

Me: Okay, okay. I will try to focus on that in my brain.

*Jack: You are creating lovely memories for both of us.*

Me: I don't do this alone, and you know that; it is <u>us</u>, <u>always us</u>.

*Jack: Yes Sweetheart, <u>it is always us and God</u>. <u>WE ARE ALL ONE, and this is what you need to accept</u>.*

Me: <u>God, tell me, show me how to do this</u> – to let go of what was, when it was so perfect for me. I have absolutely no complaints about how my life was with Jack.

**GOD: My Child. Your life is still with your Jack, but don't forget to include me! This you know of but sometimes forget. <u>As your beloved tells you, WE ARE ALL ONE, and the strength is in this knowing</u>. He goes with you everywhere as do I. <u>You are never alone. Your pleasure is our pleasure.</u>**

Later that morning I had been directed to unpacking Jack's suitcase, jammed full of personal treasures, that I had placed immediately after his transition – I had no idea 'why' at that time that I did this – but I remember my brain had me planning to burn everything in this suitcase (with me) when my time came.

Me: Today I see, boy am I in Divine Order – I would say so! It's kind of crazy-fun finding so many of our things that I had packed away and am now choosing to put back on the shelf. I am obviously in a different space now because I don't want to destroy anything. Guess what, I have found all of our love letters from each other to each other – and it is wonderful for me. I found several lovely notes from your mother and father to me – I am pretty sure they approved of me.

*Jack: No question. They were relieved that I was 'off the streets' so-to-speak.*

Me: It has been like Christmas and birthday all on the same day today, because I found so many beautiful things you had bought me that I was hiding and had actually planned to burn. I was obviously crazy when I did this (understand, this packing of Jack's traveling suitcase had occurred immediately after his transition when I was beside myself with grief) stuffing things into the suitcase for destroying, when I died! I am so happy to have found them again and am recalling memories of the days you had bought them for me before **CAT HAVEN** was born, and you had surprised me. Beautiful, silver earrings of cats that you should never have bought – for we did not have money for such luxuries. Now so much of what was, still is! I had it all hidden away, and I cannot find a sensible answer to any of my own questions as to why I did this.

*Jack: Don't worry Baby, I am thrilled to hear of your happy findings this morning, and yes, I remember my happy thoughts when I bought them for you. Joys relived, joys relived.*

Me: I found pretty things I had looked for and wondered about and now I have them again. I am grateful for the things and the memories, mostly the memories. By the way, I found my wedding vows to you, in this suitcase. I believe I will make them part of this, our third and final book. Yours to me are clearly displayed on the back cover of our first book, Listen, I'm Still Here, Part I.

§

150

## SEPTEMBER 15, 2013 – 11:35 P.M.
### You were so romantic

Me: I am in my bed – which is 'in your chair' in your *Reading Room*, looking at the magnificent picture/poster you brought back from Boston on the short trip that you took when we first met (you will remember is hanging on the wall) – such a romantic vision. We both know what the photograph is for. It definitely out-pictured you and I and our connection even at the early stage of togetherness, and our future together with so many open doors revealed ahead of us. This picture, on this night, brings back memories of the beautiful things you did: the words, the compliments, the gestures – so many unique protective, loving gestures. The sweet music you heard and could not get to my ears fast enough. The gifts, so many small, simple but beautiful, thoughtful loving gifts you gave to me. No occasion, just heart gifts. God allowed you to make up for over 50 years of neglect by others in my life. You made up for all the inadequacies of others. You fulfilled me Jack, I felt regal with you. Thank you and thank you again. By the way, your Timex watch is still going strong. I have it laying across the hand-carved box we bought in Honduras the year before your transition, in which your ashes are stored (for over six years now). This box (with you in it) is sitting on the glass table in the living room next to my chair.

§

## SEPTEMBER 16, 2013
### Perfect love casts out fear

Me: Jack, you were so very sweet, so kind, so thoughtful and so original in your romantic ideas. How a man with your huge frame could be so gentle, so comforting with your thoughts and ideas is inconceivable. Your Vietnam War terror, you seemed to have let go of.

*Jack: Sweetheart, when I met you, it was easy and those previously held fears were gone. It is as remarkable to me as it is to you the power of our love – clearing the screen of all darkness. I was home with you, my dream of a red-haired woman.  You were it.  You still are it.  You were 'the light' for me.  It was God's plan and still is.* <u>*Our perfect love casts out the fear.*</u>

Me: So much fear in this world - with guns that give people false power.  Where is the love I say, where is the love?  Such a terrible shooting in Washington, D.C. today.  Why I ask?

*Jack:* <u>*You and I both know it is the fear* – *WHERE FEAR EXISTS, THERE IS NO LOVE*.</u>  *Baby, keep 'the light' around you.*

Me: <u>You could not have been any better than you were – I know this for sure.  But what is going on down here at this time, I have no idea.</u>

*Jack:* <u>*You don't have to know Sweetheart; God is in charge and all is well for you.*</u>

§

## SEPTEMBER 20, 2013
## The feeling of having enough

Me: Finally, finally – after months and months of waiting patiently for the publishing house to get our second book on the Internet, today, September 20, 2013, we finally made it!  How do you feel?

*Jack: Astonished at your accomplishment, together with your friend (Michele), who has obviously supported you all the way.  You are great working partners.  You obviously enjoy her skills and she certainly enjoys yours.  I am smiling because I have known for some time that this would come about and I hope you have felt my support in the difficult times for you.* <u>*BABY, THIS IS GOD'S WORK*.  *HE IS USING BOTH OF US SIMPLY BECAUSE HE CAN*.  *YOU ARE OPEN TO AND RECEPTIVE OF HIS DIRECTION, AND HE IS PLEASED* – *as am I*.  *My wife, my loving perfect wife is doing God's Will and I am fulfilled by this accomplishment*.</u>

Me: Jack, it does not come about without you.

*Jack: Remember now,* <u>*it is your attentiveness that reaches and responds that is the main source of the journey*.  *YOU MAKE IT HAPPEN* – *don't forget that*.  *I AM HERE, AS ARE SO MANY OTHERS, WHO LONG TO MAKE THE CONNECTION THAT WE HAVE*.  *THEY TRY AND TRY BUT ARE NOT RECEIVED*.</u>

*Thank you for making my continuous journey so pleasing – so*
*satisfying. Life on earth for me had little satisfaction until you.*
Me: Although there are billions of people in the world; when I saw on
the Internet that 14 people had responded to us (and our second book)
– I felt rich!

*Jack: Good girl, my sweet wife and companion forever more. Your*
*joys have only just begun.*
Me: It is like all those years ago when we had $7,000 upon your
return from working in Lake Havasu for almost a year – it's the same
feeling. It is the "I have enough, feeling" when in the scheme of
things, it is so little – but it is the feeling. Some people never have the
feeling, and I am grateful that I do. Lucky 14 – when I first looked on
the Internet, it was 11, and the next time it was 14 – not millions, just
14!! What a simpleton I am!

*Jack: Oh no, how simply wonderful and perfect you are. You*
*always pleased me on how simple it was to please you – what simple*
*gifts made you so happy.*
Me: No one will ever know how you made up for so many years of
'nothing'. You still make up for years of nothing with your continued
praise of me.

*Jack: Sweetheart, it is my joy to make you smile for you continue to*
*do so much that makes me happy and oh so proud.*
Me: Oh by the way, this was indeed a perfect day for we had 4 inches
of rain in the famous rain gauge you bought me. The creek is now
flowing, and the well is recharging. The lakes that are so many feet
down did go up a few inches today. A good day.

*Jack: I am so glad for you are certainly deserving.*
Me: Let it be known, I want 'God ideas', not good ideas.

*Jack: They are yours My Love, each and every day.*
Me: I AM LEARNING THAT ANY TIME I PUT 'SELF-EFFORT'
INTO MY PLANS, GOD STOPS HIS HELP. I AM WANTING TO
ALLOW GOD TO DO HIS WORK, HIS WAY.

*Jack: Good girl, you are really seeing the truth. **YOU MUST***
***ALLOW HIM TO HELP YOU, TO LEAD YOU. WE MUST***
***COMPLETELY DIE AND ALLOW HIM TO DO FOR US.** As I*
*have said before, it is easy.*

§

## SEPTEMBER 23, 2013
## My disappointment

*I was mulling around in my mind how disappointed I was at people not even reading the books I had <u>given</u>:*
**Jack: Just remember one thing Baby, the <u>right</u> people will read it.**

§

# CHAPTER 13
## 2013

# CHANGING MY WORLD
## – AS I GROW

**6th year of conversation after Jack's transition**

## ILLUMINATION

*Death does not separate us from those we love.*
*It deepens our union with God and with each other*

*-- Author Unknown*

## SEPTEMBER 24, 2013 – 7:40 A.M.
## CHANGING my world as I grow

Me: Oh Jack!

My Jack!

My beloved Jack!

This morning it is cool, the third day of Fall, and I am sitting in our *Meditation Room* in your favorite massaging lounger viewing a poster you gave me 25 years ago entitled "CHANGING my world as I grow". On this poster, there are five pictures of a rose – from the first bud just sprouting above the ground to the full blown, fully grown beautiful, magnificent velvet petals of a rose – which you know exudes the powerful, distinguishable rose fragrance (you can feel it from the picture). I think I am there – fully grown that is – at least on some days! I think today might be one of them. This fully grown awareness may not last, but I am aware of its existence more frequently of late.

Almost 50 years now of focus, concentration on some level of growth, personal improvement, knowing who is in charge, listening, extending patience to myself and others, doing what is right, serving others (especially the smallest of creatures), understanding that The God in all life matters and seeing The God in all life with deep gratitude for the SEEING and the KNOWING that there is a Divine Order to our lives – God is in charge, and all is well.

Your very first gift to me has significant meaning right now, and you were wise in your choice of this gift. You were a man of knowing, you were a man of wisdom – perhaps beyond your years, because I have your writings of when you were 12 years old, and they reveal this depth of your soul's knowing. I am a very lucky girl, and richly blessed, and yes my world is changing as I grow. My present lesson is to ACCEPT those changes because I now know you are with me all the way.

*Jack: You are so right and once again, I am so pleased with your recognition of the process. Understand that you are not coming to the end of anything, it is just the beginning. I know, I see, I feel your fear of ending. There is no ending Baby, you may think so, but that is not so; where I am, I see even for me, so much more than*

*I ever knew.  It is a vast new world out here.  Flying is a fabulous state to be.  Yes My Love, I am everywhere present as is God.  When we let go of preconceived notions of life's limited experiences, we elevate to indescribable heights – worlds above worlds.  I see it all now, and there are so many universes beyond anything written in the books of life.  It is so happy and unlimited where I am; yet in an instant, I can be anywhere I am needed.  Over here, we all work in a 'holy instant' where God wishes us to be.  God is in charge Sweetie, TRUST HIM and that is all you have to do.*

Me: That's interesting.  I read your message of this morning to Paul Minar, and he said you had a lot to say today.

*Jack: That's because you were in the right space for listening, and I don't want to talk to deaf ears!*

§

## SEPTEMBER 28, 2013 – 4:38 P.M.
### I've got what it takes

Me: I just woke up from a nap with the deep realization that I know who I am, I am God's child, and I've got what it takes to survive anything.  No matter how difficult life seems to be sometimes, when things don't flow or go easily, all IS well.  I've got what it takes in this world full of fear, I have got God, and every fiber of my being knows it.  I didn't used to know it; Jack always did; now I do too.

   The threat of the government closing down, the nation running out of money, political parties arguing (people we chose as our leaders – imagine that!), what a world.  Anyone can be afraid if they choose.  I don't choose because I am not of this world.

*Jack: Again I say, good girl to my wife.  No Sweetheart, you have nothing to worry about because GOD IS IN CHARGE FOR THOSE WHO BELIEVE, and FOR THOSE WHO BELIEVE, ALL IS WELL.  His light shines upon you, all around and beams from within you.  You shine it everywhere you go and upon everyone you meet.  What a light you are and how blessed you make our loving Father and me.*

§

## OCTOBER 1, 2013
## My gratitude

Me: Oh God, I am so grateful for everything I have and everything I see and everything I know is coming to me.
*Jack: You have got the picture Baby, with clarity.*

§

## OCTOBER 6, 2013

Me: Jack, you were the best that a man could be, the best that a husband could be, the best that a loving friend and companion could be. I am so blessed. God brought you to me.
*Jack: You know my answer – the best attracts the best.*
Me: You are the best Jack.
*Jack: That is because you are.*

§

## OCTOBER 8, 2013 – 8: 16 A.M.
## Life can be good

Last night a friendly fox I saw and this morning, wow, what a beautiful sight for me. A huge crow eating just outside the house, some dog food I had placed for the raccoons. He ate several pieces and then flew to the rain-filled bird bath to drink water. I watched this as I was listening to hootie owls who were very energetic today also. And there in the background from someone else's property, I could hear hens 'cockadoodling'. I love country life.

§

## WEDNESDAY, OCTOBER 17, 2013
## A beautiful day today

Me: Jack, today was such a lovely day. It has not been an easy thing to arrange schedules for Kristina and I to get together, but today it happened. (Kristina worked for us for six years when the cats were

159

kittens; she is now a grown, young lady.)  It was simply fascinating today to witness how many of the remaining cats recognized her voice and presence. What I think I am trying to say is that the memory of some of the cats is quite astonishing.  Once again, it has been months, in fact when I think back almost a year since Kristina last came to visit, and yet some of them still remember her. ***Betina, Spike, Bitsy*** and ***Neecy*** came running - so thrilling to witness.  A few required a repetition of her speaking for the memory recall to hone in, but it was there – it <u>was there.</u>

*Jack: Sweetheart, I was there through it all, and she certainly appreciates you and your goodness at this time.  She has been through many experiences for growth since working with us and is now able to understand things you tell her.  It was indeed a lovely morning for all of you.  Don't forget to include me.  The transference of gifts was good, and I know it was appreciated.  Good stimulation for the cats, very good.  Her presence woke some of them up.*

§

**OCTOBER 19, 2013**

Me: I want the world to know about what you have taught me.

*Jack: And what you have learned.*

Me: I am so sorry I was not all I could have been for you.

*Jack: Sweetheart, you were exactly what I needed, just the way you were.*

Me: Thank you God for eyes that see all that you have given me, and Jack, you did not waste a minute of your time here on Earth that I did not appreciate.

*Jack: Sweetheart, I know.  You're appreciation was my blessing.*

§

# CHAPTER 14
## 2013

# GOD GIVES US LIFE
## – BUT WE MAKE OURSELVES

**6<sup>th</sup> year of conversation after Jack's transition**

# ILLUMINATION

*I do not pray for the results*
*for only God knows*
*what they may be.*
*But I pray for the energy*
*to sustain my effort*
*toward the results*
*by way of right action.*

*I do not pray to be spared failure*
*for who can know*
*what opportunity*
*an adversity may mask?*
*But I pray for the courage*
*to overcome failure*
*again and again if necessary.*

*I do not pray for specific success or achievement*
*But only for those signposts*
*that I am indeed following my path*
*and that my life is of use to others.*

*I do not pray as a means of asking for*
*But of giving thanks,*
*for prayer is the effect of thought*
*which occupies time and space*
*and having seen*
*what therefore must be*
*Should I be less than thankful?*

*-- Author Unknown*

**OCTOBER 24, 2013**
**God gives us life, but "we make ourselves"**

*I was having favorable memory recall of some of Jack's beautiful caring for me and said out loud:*

Me: You made a good one God when you made my Jack.
**GOD: No My Child, he made himself.**

**To the World I Say**

I was gazing at the full moon at 6:30 A.M. this morning – while walking up the driveway from the first cat feeding of the day for the cats who don't choose to go into the comfort of the buildings, but would rather sleep in the hay placed in the many dogloos outside. It is their choice, and I have learned to allow that because forcing them to be in buildings for some is an unhappy situation. As I was walking, I had fond memories while looking at this magnificent moon, of Jack's wisdom which he always shared with grace. This man, my husband, knew the stars above, and taught me so much as we lay in a hammock in Llano, Texas and gazed! He knew of the oceans below for he was an Aries, passionate about the water. He was a certified diver and interested in all water sports. He was always willing to share his knowledge, and I certainly listened but I was afraid of the water. When I was 11 years old, after the ending of World War II and on a holiday at the coast of England – when some part of Britain's coast line were still surrounded with barbed wire, yet opened for swimming – I almost drowned while floating in a huge automobile tire inner-tube. I was very small in stature and because of the war had never been to a swimming pool and had never learned to swim. At that moment when I slipped into the water while out of my depth, my entire life went before me at this early age. Miraculously I survived. However, fear of water never left me until Jack and his support, and ocean cruises became fun with him beside me. Yes I had fear of the water for years, and our fears prevent us from learning and growing.

Jack knew the soil of the earth, and in the late 80s had one of the biggest organic gardens in the state of Texas on his parents land – (again, in Llano) which had not been toiled for over 50 years (see *Listen, I'm Still Here* – Part I).

He knew the mountains and had camped and climbed. I was afraid of heights. He knew the mysteries of life's meaning. He had questioned, he had explored and sought answers. HE WAS A 'WHOLE MAN', even when I first met him. He was ready for me; he was intellectually, physically, emotionally and spiritually prepared – he was without question, 'whole'.

As God once said, 'he made himself'. My Jack could take you to high places while doing mundane tasks (see *I'm Always Here* – Part II). And as for me, I'm still in the process of becoming whole. Being left alone – is the Divine Plan for me to accomplish this. I know it. I was certainly on the right path when Jack and I first met, there's no doubt about that or I would not have been deserving of so much or understanding of so much or willing to listen to so much – Jack was so much. He was younger in years, but so much wiser.

All of this memory recall from looking at the moon!

§

**To the World I Say – I KNOW PAIN**

Fifty years of volunteering my time, giving my things, many trips out at night to help others and experiencing that others were not there for me when I had needs and was hurting – I know pain. I know pain of no support; I know pain of many things.

I know the pain of betrayal by friends of 30 years who made promises but did not keep them and family of more than 50 years. I know that level of disappointment and have learned that we should never do or give with expectation of reward.

We should never judge another because we do not know of their karmic debt, as we do not realize the debts we are paying. All is fair when we work for you dear God. I believe we have debts to pay from other lives <u>when we were not fair, not kind</u> – our failures known only to God. We must forgive as we ask for forgiveness – in Jesus name – and so it is. <u>WE ARE TO JUST KEEP POLISHING OUR SOUL</u>.

**WORTHY OF THOUGHT – To name a few, I know the pain of:**

- ❖ Shame
- ❖ War - Bombings
- ❖ Hunger
- ❖ Loss of friends as a child, in War
- ❖ Personal injury by others
- ❖ Infection
- ❖ Bullying
- ❖ Verbal Assault
- ❖ Embarrassment

- ❖ Physical Assault
- ❖ Sickness
- ❖ Giving birth
- ❖ Home flooding
- ❖ Rape by persons unknown and known
- ❖ Rejection
- ❖ Divorce
- ❖ No work
- ❖ No money

- ❖ No heat/AC
- ❖ Home Invasion/ Burglary
- ❖ Loss of valuables, including animals
- ❖ Betrayal, friends and family
- ❖ Loss of 70+ pets
- ❖ Age Discrimination
- ❖ Husband's transition

<u>However, my feeling is the 'pain of regret' – can be worse than the pain of pain for there is no cure; there is no remedy; IT'S TOO LATE</u>. However, I have come through it all – stronger, smarter, more cautious, more appreciative, more thoughtful, more grateful, more generous and more joyful. The pain didn't destroy or make me hateful, not at all. I believe I am a better person, a more rounded person, more understanding, more accepting and certainly more loving. **I KNOW WHO I AM. I know who is in charge of my life and how to get on His side – easy, through Jesus Christ. I am now a WINNER, and I know it.**

§

**OCTOBER 27, 2013**
**I was over the moon this morning**

Me: Not that I need to tell you anything, because I now know you know it all. Yes, you are 'a know it all'! However, since I am still here in the earthly realm, allow me to express myself.
*Jack: Most certainly, because I enjoy your enthusiasm, and it is abundant.*
Me: Well, our first tad of recognition from the publishing house came

165

today and news that our book, *I'm Always Here*, Part II (which as you know is our second book) will be featured early next year in a special book festival here in Austin. We will be featured authors, imagine that!

I was over the moon this morning when I retrieved a voicemail message of yesterday from one of the lovely ladies with Hay House Publishing who informed me of this. I know that you know why I was so excited because never before you, was I told I could do anything – never. In my 52 years of life – this time around, had I ever received words of encouragement or compliments on my abilities – until YOU. You made up for the years of lack in all ways in my life. (Of course I am very well aware it is the Father within that brings forth the wisdom, and I know my gift is the love for Him and for you, that allows this.)

*Jack: I told you recently there is no ending for you My Love. It is just the beginning, and yes I understand completely your childlike reaction. It is beautiful to witness you so joyful and alive. I am happy and yes, <u>I am certainly over the moon with you. YOU ARE NEVER ANYWHERE THAT I AM NOT.</u>*

Me: Your heart and my heart are one heart, and when yours died, part of mine died also.

*Jack: Not so. God holds us together.*

Me: Thank you God for a man who never judged me.

*Jack: It was easy Baby, so easy.*

§

**OCTOBER 28, 2013 – 9:52 A.M.**
**The body IS the learning device of the mind**
*I AM therefore, I think. I think, therefore I AM.*

**To the World I Say**

While standing at the kitchen sink, I was mulling over in my mind the thought process of the incredible opportunity being afforded to Jack and me as co-authors of our second book, *I'm Always Here*, Part II and the fact that we were going to be featured authors in an up-

166

coming book festival in 2014, here in Texas. This was a decision made by the publishing house. What an opportunity! Huge opportunity – and we had been selected. Who did we think or certainly who did I think I was? Of course it is the Father within who does this work, this writing is through me, yet it is for me to learn and to grow from and hopefully for others too. IT IS OUR MESSAGE OF LOVE.

I was feeling pain, intensified pain in my left knee – which has bothered me ever since my beloved Jack moved onward and upward. In the past, I had blamed everything – the weather, my moving too fast, doing too much, and yet here I was STANDING STILL and only my mind was in gear. I was thinking about this fabulous, once in a lifetime opportunity, to be featured by this world-renowned publishing house (Hay House). The pain became so red hot intense, so gripping, so debilitating – I knew something was happening for me (I actually laughed out loud), and that I needed to get my mind into gear and on the right track. I knew everything that was happening was for me to unravel myself from me. I have learned that the body IS the learning device of the mind. Of course, Louise Hays' dilapidated book (dilapidated by me) was sought after.

> "Left knee joint: represents changes in direction
> in life and the ease of these movements.
>
> Pride and ego: that I be flexible and flowing
> and not stubborn with an inability to bend
> - that I learn to give in, that I extend forgiveness,
> understanding and compassion, that I bend
> and flow with ease – and all will be well.
>
> Leg problems: represent fear of the future that I must move
> forward with confidence knowing all IS well in my future."

At 78 years of age, I suspect it is natural to have some fear of the future – what remains that is, and that there might not be enough of it for me. I was doubting and certainly not trusting. Well, the words through Ms. Hay soon had my mind in proper alignment and thereafter my body. I was obviously not trusting the Divine Order of things. I was still hearing my mother's voice with, "You cannot do that."

"Mother, I CAN DO IT, and I WILL because I AM – and then I saw my notes and recognized that the name of the book festival is "I CAN DO IT"!

*Jack: You are incredible in your choice for learning. I applaud your efforts. We are close today, very close. Just let go of your remaining doubts for you are in the arms of the angels and of me. Trust that you will be free of lingering pain.*
Me: No kidding, the intense pain is gone.

*Let it be known I had no idea that I CAN DO IT was the name of the conference.*

## SAME DAY – 2:50 P.M.

Me: Oh my goodness Jack, I have just put the phone down from the publishing house, and their overview of cost and expectations of me for this opportunity. It is quite simple, but quite expensive. I signed up immediately for one day, and I'm leaving it up to you to tell me what to do for the second day. Guess what, it happens to be June 7 and 8; June 7 being the anniversary of our very first conversation, ever! Hay House has apparently only 12 slots for authors from all over the world. Imagine that! It would be great to feel comfortable taking a second day because we could promote our two books, but I'm not sure. I am not sure, because I don't know whether it will be beneficial to promote both books. It sounds good, but I am not sure at all.
*Jack: I will put you straight. Go for it while you have the chance. Honestly, it will pay for itself.*
Me: The young woman selling me this opportunity said that most people pay more than the cost of the promotion for their travel plans, and I don't have to pay anything for travel or hotel because it is happening in my town.
*Jack: It sounds absolutely perfect for us.*

Me: I told the marketing gal, Fatima, that my main purpose for being on this Earth plane is the Mission of **CAT HAVEN** and the care of the animals, and the Message is secondary, and hopefully will aid in the care of these beautiful creatures. I looked outside and cannot count how many doe are resting on the hillside outside *The House* and especially close to your room. It is just too beautiful for words and confirms to my heart that the Mission is #1 for me.

*Jack: Yes, but the support of it will be affected by the books. Don't hesitate and don't worry. I am here, always here.*

Me: Are the animals saying, "Don't forget us, we come first"? I think you will have to give me a dream to confirm what I am supposed to do. It is 85 degrees today, and these babies on our hillside all look worn out. The recent storms have the swamp area where they usually sit looking like a lake, and so I am feeling that they don't have their usual resting place available and I am certainly happy to have them near to me. They are feasting on acorns which despite the serious drought are prolific this year, and especially in the area where they are sitting.

Shakti said she would go with me to the book signing festival in 2014.

*Jack: Of course, anyone in their right mind would go.*

§

### OCTOBER 30, 2013 – 6:15 A.M.
### My first smile of my day

Today my first smile of the day was at *Rose* – it's raining today, but *Rose* was sitting on the high screen you built by the front gate – in the rain. She is still obviously very alert and agile – nice to smile so early in the day. I love *Rose* even though after all these years she is still so full of fear; she seldom comes to me, does not allow petting, just wants food.

169

**SAME DAY – 10:25 A.M.**
**There's not enough LOVE in the world**

Me: *Mittens* is such a beautiful cat Jack. He used to be so frightened
of everything, but the years of love and companionship from his loyal
friend *Spike* have him a beautiful little soul now. He weighs almost
nothing, yet he bounds up the driveway every day to see me and to
get his favorite cat milk. He jumps up on the back deck bench, and
I can hear his cry – while I am inside *The House* – and if I have not
already placed what he wants on the bench, I always immediately hop
to it. He is sleeping on a chair outside our house door right now; his
tummy is full, so what else should he do while it's raining! He knows
he is loved and returns it gracefully. Yes, we love each other, and it
is simply wonderful. His claws have hurt me on many occasions, but
he won't stay still long enough for me to clip them. And so, there is
total forgiveness between us. Remember, *Mittens*, *Happy*, *Dimples*
and *Strom* are all from the same litter found on the neighbor's land.
Very slim cats, very scared cats – *Dimples* and *Strom* are still here but
'untouchable'. *Happy* moved on a year ago, and *Mittens* is the most
spiritually developed little creature of their family. I endeavor to treat
them all the same, but they don't respond the same. My reward is
when they recognize my gift to them – MY LOVE.
 SO MANY PEOPLE DON'T RECOGNIZE LOVE EITHER,
AND THAT SEEMS TO BE THE PROBLEM IN THE WORLD –
THERE'S NOT ENOUGH LOVE.

§

**OCTOBER 31, 2013 – 7:10 A.M.**
**A Historic Flood**

A historic flood here this date, yet a beautiful fox showed its face by
the *Bathhouse*. He or she is obviously on this side of the creek which
presently has white caps on it, but this water is recharging our well,
and that is the best news.

§

## NOVEMBER 1, 2013 – 7:50 P.M.
### Flooding

Me: Still not a good day because the flooding has been so heavy, Marie and I had to walk around here in waters so deep, it required wading boots.

Today, our *Mattie* is not feeling good at all. She keeps going outside of her building onto the protected, elevated boardwalks (that we define as cat runs) she enjoys so much, but due to the flooding – she is getting her feet wet, and it is cold. She's not eating or drinking, and so tomorrow our wonderful veterinarian, Dr. Stried is coming to put her to sleep. I have spent ages in the *Ruffhouse* this evening trying to comfort *Mattie*, certainly holding and petting her, but our *Groucho* has demanded his share of attention too – which, I have not minded at all. His time on Earth is limited now, for he is very thin although he eats huge amounts of canned foods. I just keep it coming, never giving thought to expense. Everything is as it should be, although I don't like it – I accept it. Keep watching us.
*Jack: Of course My Love, of course.*

§

## NOVEMBER 2, 2013 – 12:45 P.M.
### Our *Mattie* will be on her way to Heaven this afternoon

Me: Oh Jack, I know everything's as it should be, but I am already missing *Mattie* who will be on her way to Heaven this afternoon. She has been such a good kitty (one of the litters we rescued that were trapped at a local Shamrock gas station so many years ago). *Marie*, her twin sister, joined you about a year ago. Her brother *Rocky* left us after only three years of being here. Do you remember?
*Jack: Baby of course I do.*
Me: Dr. Stried performed an autopsy on *Rocky* at that time because he was alive at 8 A.M. and dead at 8:15 A.M. (The autopsy revealed he had a heart condition.)

*Maudie* (one of the five cats from this original litter; is a dark, long-haired Calico who looks the most like *Brandy* – the cat in

171

whose memory **CAT HAVEN** was built almost 20 years ago) looks wonderful and feels good to the touch with her weight and fur. She allows petting and holding.

*Jack: Sweetheart, I see Brandy from time to time when I focus on the gathering of them all.*

> Here is a funny story about **Zeppo** (brother to **Harpo** and **Groucho**) – he likes **Mittens** and wants to go into the Bunkhouse building where **Mittens** lives. I placed him with his friend after years of his living alone because he never liked other cats and showed his dislike in an unlikable manner. His attitude revealed this affection; you see **_LOVE CHANGES ALL OF US_**.

§

**SAME DAY – 4;10 P.M.**

Me: Our wonderful veterinarian just left the property. Our *Mattie* is now lying on a warm pink blanket covering a comfortable round bed, with another layer of pink blanket and lace over her. She is lying in state on the floor in her building, the *Ruffhouse*, so the remaining cats can comfort her. Tomorrow I will bury her in the cemetery on the land. She was such a good little lady to the very end; today she got up from her nap in the **CAT HAVEN** building, used the litter box and walked down the hall to the counter where I picked her up in my arms, and Dr. Stried gave her medicine to sleep. She is with you now.

*Jack: She certainly is, and there are many of her friends to greet her. I promise you, she is not alone.*

Me: I did a little bragging to our vet today about the opportunity for our books being featured in a Hay House book festival next year, here in town.

*Jack: Brag all you want, you certainly deserve.*

Me: That is sort of what the veterinarian said also.

*Jack: I am glad, because your effort is what has brought this opportunity about.*

Me: And I say, it was your presence in Spirit form 'for all the world to see' on the video (YouTube – Dorothy and Jack Farley, *I'm Always Here*), that brought this opportunity to us.

172

*Jack: Baby, <u>we are and always will be a team</u> – <u>a perfect team doing</u>*
*<u>God's Will</u>.*

§

## NOVEMBER 3, 2013
### Our *Mattie* is in Heaven now
*Mattie, a long-haired gray female; her twin sister was* **Marie** *who*
*transitioned about a year ago.*

> Her precious, precious frail body, but strong little spirit, is safe,
> secure and at peace now, and she is lying with her friends up the
> hill in our cat cemetery near *Trough I*. René, Maria and I buried
> her today.

§

## SATURDAY, NOVEMBER 9, 2013 – 4:22 P.M.
### Too funny for words
Me: I was about to close the back portico doors, because although
it has been a beautiful day – considering it is November and the
afternoon temperature has been in the 70s, I felt the evening chill and
the need to close the glass doors. I could hear this unusual sound
of 'crunching', of wood and leaves, and then I stopped to look and
listen. Guess what, there were several deer actually walking on our
high back wood deck eating acorns. (Understand, the deck has access
to the ground on one end, the end closest to our house – by only a
few inches; however, the back part of that deck is three to four feet
off the ground and certainly not accessible!) I halted the closing of
the glass doors and watched in wonderment at the audacity of these
remarkable creatures in their search for the Fall food. In spite of the
drought, we have had a bumper crop of acorns this year. Thank you
God, the provider of such good things when we least expect it. We
are blessed Jack, constantly. Oh my gosh – in my second attempt to
close the doors, I see that these huge 'ladies' are so close to our house,
wandering among the rocks and fountains and eating these treasures.
Jack, they are huge, so majestic; the *Fox Feed Table* that you built is
dwarfed by their majestic stature.

*Jack: Thank you Sweetheart for the description. I see it all so clearly and am as thrilled for you as you are. Yes we love the creatures, truly love them.*

**4:39 P.M.**
Me: A final attempt before I go down to *The Village* to put our babies to bed, and I witnessed several squirrels scurrying in between the deer. Everyone is happy here.
*Jack: Good girl, you are doing such a great job. I glow with gratitude and pride.*

**6:15 P.M.**
Me: Well, I have just fed our spoiled kitties their final meal for this day – they love the canned food now better than the dry, and of course this is what they get. The very best, fancy feast and as much as they want! Some of them are such chunky monkeys, and I hold the plate right up to their faces so they can eat and not get out of their warm beds. I'm sure it is not the best thing for them, but I want them happy and so this is what I do. I actually laugh out loud at the preposterousness of it all, but our babies are happy and therefore, so am I. No regrets that I could have done more for them, for that is certainly not the case. That pain for me is the worst kind of pain, and I choose to avoid it at all costs.

 For your information Jack, Lou (Jack's trim carpenter who has been so loyal in his support of me and **CAT HAVEN** Trust) recently cut pieces of the plastic wood for replacing wood signage that you originally made, and he is taking off the original metal signs and joining them together with the plastic wood for permanency. These new and beautiful signs, indicating for example 'Deer Crossing Pathways' will last forever, or so I hope. The wooden signs you originally placed have been there for 15 years at least, but they were looking a little weathered. It is my intention to maintain perfection here in the landscaping. Not an easy task with floods and droughts, but I do my best.
*Jack: I know that, for you always did, but please I implore you to not hurt yourself for the sake of the land.*

Me: I plan to work on our third book this weekend, *Everlasting Love – That is,* and make corrections to the 100 pages we have completed so far.

*Jack: I definitely approve of the title.*

Me: Well, when you told me, *"we have the highest and deepest love that two souls can bathe in"* – this title came immediately to mind.

*Jack: Good job – your thinking is certainly in line with God's choices.*

Me: That's what I want more than anything – to please Him.

*Jack: You do. Never doubt that.*

Me: Well among the dry dog, cat food with milk bones the raccoons will be feeding on tonight; there are some small cups of applesauce that I found to be totally disgusting.

*Jack: Funny. They will love it, you can bet on that.*

Me: It is so interesting isn't. <u>You can be turned inside out, upside down with love and yet still more can flow from you.</u>

*Jack: Of course, <u>as you grow you know this is what happens. You become more, and you are able to love more. It is 'in the becoming' that the beauty comes forth. It is endless – highest and deepest, remember that</u>!*

§

## NOVEMBER 10, 2013 – 7:55 A.M.
### Deep thoughts

Me: I was having really deep thoughts about what you and I are doing, writing books together, being acknowledged by the biggest metaphysical publishing house in the country, being given 'a once in a lifetime' opportunity to present our books to the public and saying to myself that I would have to do this 'without you' is not true, because you are in a higher place to guide me.

*Jack: True*

Me: This is crazy!

*Jack: I know, but isn't it wonderful. <u>GOD TRUSTS US TO GIVE OUR MESSAGE TO THE PEOPLE. THEY WILL LEARN FROM US THAT THERE IS NO DEATH ENDING, BUT THAT LIFE</u>*

*AND LIVING GO ON AND ON IN ANOTHER DIMENSION.*
*LEARNING NEVER CEASES, BECAUSE I AM STILL*
*LEARNING WHERE I AM NOW.* I particularly learn through
you. *I HAVE LEARNED THAT I TOO COULD HAVE BEEN*
*BETTER, AND I COULD HAVE DONE MORE TO BE A BETTER*
*PERSON AND A BETTER HUSBAND. I SEE IT NOW, BUT ON*
*EARTH, MY REMAINING PRIDE WOULD NOT ALLOW IT.*

§

## NOVEMBER 14, 2013
### This is all new to me

Me: For 25 years, you have been in my life, this time around. I
am now realizing that because no one had ever been so kind, so
thoughtful, so loving and giving with their remembrances of our
special occasions, I was always over the moon with excitement
and joy at your goodness. Because of this reaction from me for
doing things you had always done for others and as a result of my
enthusiastic appreciation of you, you were encouraged to do more
thoughtful, kind and loving things – because this is what you had
always wanted – grateful reaction – am I right?
*Jack: Absolutely. It was my pleasure to give you pleasure. I believe*
*it was my nature, but no one had ever responded with such gratitude*
*until you. Yes, My Love, we were made for each other.*
Me: Well no one had ever given to me until you, absolutely no one.
Not even a flower. I could never quite believe your attention and
somehow felt underserving.
*Jack: Banish that thought forever more. We made everything right*
*for each other, and that's the truth. I love you highest and deepest,*
*and that is the truth also.*

### LATER –9:35 A.M.
Me: Jack, today because I am thinking about what is happening for
us, I am giggling. I cannot quite grasp it, us, featured authors at a
book signing (a Hay House book signing). How is this possible? Yet,
I think I am proving a point – at least to myself. WHEN YOU 'STAY

IN THE LOVE VIBRATION', ENDEAVORING TO DO GOD'S WILL, YOU CANNOT FAIL. It is not easy; at times it seems impossible, because right now it is a bit of a struggle for me; yet, in the KNOWING, I have comfort. It will happen – I love what I need to do to maintain our Mission, and our Message will be delivered to the people.

*Jack: I am so proud of you – and yes you are right, everything is a done deal.*

Me: This is all new to me, I am 78 years young and this is new to me. You have to be in the realm of receptivity, before you receive.

**SAME DAY**
**Let's not forget – today is our wedding anniversary – and you are still making things happen for us!!**

*(You are bringing things together from your new realm – YOU are making things happen for us.)*

Me: Oh my Jack, my humble and taciturn, eternal partner and loving husband – YOU are bringing things together for us from your new realm. Imagine that! My gentle, giant of a man, you are out there, and hundreds of people have already witnessed your Spirit form. I hope you are enjoying your demonstration of Spirit, as much as I am.

*Jack: JUST DOING GOD'S WILL BABY. I GO WHERE HE TELLS ME. IT IS NOT ALWAYS A CHOICE I MAKE ALONE; IT IS HIS CHOICE FOR ME TO BE WHERE THERE IS NEED, FOR YOU, OR FOR OTHERS. REMEMBER NOW, I WORK FOR HIM, AS DO YOU AND ALL OF US. HIS WILL, NOT OURS, BE DONE BUT NEVERTHELESS, I AM HAPPY WHEN YOU ARE.*

§

**NOVEMBER 16, 2013**
**Today you are here in vibrant, butterfly form with others**

Me: Thank you so much for revealing your spirit this morning in the bright sunshine on the driveway in front of our Tahoe automobile.

René was here when I screeched out, "My husband's spirit is here!"
This has not occurred now in several weeks, and I was so happy.

*Jack: Yes, Sweet One, I know you were happy, and yes I brought some of our babies.*

## To the World I Say

We have access to it all. We may not have everything we want right now, but we have access to it, through Jesus Christ. We may not know it all, but we have access to it, that Divine Wisdom.

*Jack: It is in the knowing that we have it. It is ours, it is yours. We have entitlement to our heart's desire through Jesus Christ. Accept it, be ready to receive it, it is guaranteed. Through Jesus, let go and receive.*

§

## NOVEMBER 24, 2013
## The consolation of eternal life

Me: This day I had received in the mail a small pamphlet from a mission I donate to, wherein there is confirmation of my recent learning – that is in these past 7 years since the transition of my beloved husband that we are not separated from those who have gone to the other side before us.

*Jack: Absolutely My Love. You know the truth of when and how our Divine Creator has us in His palm. May this peace, His peace, bring you comfort. This is what I want for you as I always did. Your comfort is mine. Remember that. Always was, and always will be.*

Me: You are the best Jack.

*Jack: No, WE are. Our oneness with God is all there is, and that is the best – always.*

§

## NOVEMBER 27, 2013 – 12:20 P.M.
### I continue to grow more proud of our *Mittens*

Jack, I know I talk about him often, but I cannot cease my wonderment at him and how he has grown from such a fearful little guy to such a beautiful, loving healthy-looking boy cat. This year, he has literally eaten himself to health. I feed him whatever and whenever he wants, and he drinks cat milk by the bowl. He has flesh on his little body now, and his fur shines even though he has a saliva problem which prevents him from cleaning his body perfectly. To me, it is perfect, and I love him completely. Every day he walks to our house, some 600 to 700 feet roundtrip, to eat whatever I put out. He sits on the chair in the sunshine outside the door and enjoys the view. Remember how he would <u>never</u> come when we called, <u>never</u> allow us to pick him up and led me a dance to get him into his building? Well, now he comes in when either Maria or I call his name. Wonderful reward for the hard work it took to get him into this receptive space. His eyes shine with a joy I never imagined!

*Zeppo* is living in the same house with him now, and they are buddies. I see *Zeppo* is happier than he has ever been. *Spike* is the third roommate and remains cool and calm at all times. He is a beautiful boy cat and most unselfish.

§

## FRIDAY, NOVEMBER 29, 2013
### Some beautiful sights today
### – God's Will for our land is being fulfilled

The weather has been pretty nasty for the past week. Heavy rain, freezing cold and strong winds, but today there is sunshine, and it will be in the 60s. I have been in our house rather than the office, because today Michele was not feeling well and did not come to work on our third book. I spent 5 hours yesterday proofing it, so I thought today would be a perfect day to clean house and as a result, I've been constantly looking out of the windows. There

179

are a lot of deer feeding today, not only eating on their foods but also eating the bird seeds, because this mixture is full of peanuts and other nuts, and they definitely like this. I heard a clatter at the *Gekko Feed Station* about 10:15 A.M. and saw a beautiful fox heading toward our house. I hastily filled a bowl with dog chow and small biscuits. Even though they know the sound of the food rattling in the bowl, this one ran away – at least for now. What I witnessed next was to me remarkable; a huge black bird I assumed to be a crow (I now believe to be a raven) was flying away with a small dog biscuit in its beak. I have never seen this before, and so the smaller bones will be served more often. What sights – not traffic, not trucks – but nature responding to our presentation of foods. I am so happy to see this.

*Jack: I know you are, and I am happy to hear about it. There is no doubt our dream of* **CAT HAVEN** *and the creation of same is God's Will for the land.*

§

# CHAPTER 15
## 2013

# WHERE WERE <u>YOU</u>, WHEN GOD FIRST HAD YOU – IN HIS PALM

6<sup>th</sup> year of conversation after Jack's transition

## ILLUMINATION

*Where were YOU, when God first had YOU*
*in His palm?*
*I'll just bet that YOU were in,*
*Vietnam.*
*In the U Minh Forest, and Cambodia*
*where OUR military were not supposed to be,*
*and there YOU were, ABANDONED –*
*immersed in the 'dirty tricks' of your government's secrecy.*

*DESERTED, alone, at age 22*
*and just what were YOU supposed to do?*
*No radio, no helicopter, no support team to help you, as promised –*
*instead, B-52 bombers surrounded your head.*
*Coordinates your skills had provided at your superior's request,*
*now had you 'an easy target' for having done your best!*

*The Naval S.E.R.E. Training, held you in good stead.*
*(Survival, Evasion, Resistance, and Escape)*
*Without this instruction, you would have been dead.*
*Your youthful attentiveness and discipline allowed you to survive*
*and with our dear God's blessing, you got out alive.*
*You had yet another mission and still – TO MEET ME!*
*There was more work for you,*
*YOU HAD TO BE FREE.*

*You honored your NAVAL promise and not one word was spoken,*
*but after 18 years of pain, your silence was broken.*
*Enemy capture, although brief,*
*had brought you years of untold grief.*
*(Against your will, you had been forced to kill.)*

*You went to the mountains to write of your ordeal.*
*You wrote Little Victories and expressed what was real.*
*THE TRUTH, as you lived it, no longer did you conceal.*
*With the release of this torment, you were able to heal.*

*C.I.A. code names – Tom Thatcher and such*
*proved perhaps – that YOU DID KNOW too much.*

182

## NOVEMBER 2013
### Where were you?

Where were <u>you</u> at age 22,
when the U.S. Navy and your country deserted you?
Sworn to secrecy on dangerous missions,
you did what they wanted you to, you followed orders
but were left in enemy territory – the C.I.A. and President had
betrayed you
Almost destroyed you – left you for dead
Waves of B-52 bombers surrounded your head
No radio, no helicopter to help you
All promises of support were broken to you
You miraculously made it through
But who did you turn to?

It must have been God, and you must have been in Vietnam. I know your emotional wounds were deep at what you had seen and what you had to react and respond to. I know as you expressed in your personal book, *Little Victories* (<u>your true story from the Vietnam War</u>) of your years of nightmares and pain – until you say, you had written your book to release these emotions and had met me, to restore your love for life and living.

**GOD LOVES IT WHEN WE HAVE TO DEPEND ON HIM.**
**WHEN WE HAVE LEARNED TO DEPEND ON THE**
**INVISIBLE AND TRUST WHAT WE KNOW IN**
**OUR HEARTS, IS TRUTH.**

<u>I now know what it is like being left alone and have learned to trust</u>
<u>God, for I do</u> – <u>just like you</u>.

At the time I first met Jack in June 1988, he had recently returned from the National Forest Camp Ground (Big Tesuque), Santa Fe, New Mexico where he had camped in the mountains and written his own book, *Little Victories*, in an attempt to cleanse his emotional body and release the nightmares and pain of betrayal

183

by the U.S. Navy, C.I.A. and his government. He had worked through it and was not bitter but full of love and light. He had grown through this monstrous pain of betrayal. God was pleased with him, and Jack was ready for me – the next challenge in his life!

Me: You were treated so badly by our government and came through the most beautiful man – loving, forgiving, understanding and strong.
*Jack: You were the most important part of my healing Sweetheart. You allowed me to shine, and you still do. All that I had learned, you allowed me to put into practice. You saw my growth as no one before you. We were so necessary for each other. Subliminally, God's Plan, for neither of us knew of this until now. No opportunity to boast for that is not what God wants – everything is as it should be. Our timing is perfect.*
Me: You did get into that space of perfect love, God's love – completely. THROUGH HIS LOVE FOR YOU, you found the strength to get out of the enemy's hands and miraculously found your way home. You were alone, no radio, no helicopter – in enemy territory, and yet you survived.

I came into your life when you had released the intensity of emotion that had been locked in your body for 18 years since your youth; you were 22 and now 40. (That is when we met.) The nightmares you had experienced, you told me were over once we met.
*Jack: For sure. Without doubt, my lingering dream of you, my red-headed beauty was real. THANK YOU GOD.*

**To the World I say**:

Maybe your experiences in Vietnam, deserted by your country, left to die alone in the U Minh Forest one time, and on the beaches of Cambodia – yet a second time (where U.S. Troops were not supposed to be) made you stronger, gave you meaning to live and taught you what life was about. I don't know, but this experience must have influenced your life in some deep, powerful way.

I know from some of the conversations we had about your service in Vietnam that this experience changed you, changed your thinking, changed your level of trust and opened your heart to what is really important. (Once again, you had no one) – **GOD HAD YOU IN THE PALM OF HIS HAND WHERE YOU HAD TO TRUST HIM**. You did; <u>you were 22 years of age when you were left to die alone, and I know this changed your perception of life. You were not wounded physically, but I know you were deeply wounded emotionally – betrayal is an intense lesson to overcome and when it is by your country and government, it must have been devastating</u>.

*Jack: Once I met you, I was at peace.*

§

# CHAPTER 16
# 2013

## MY JACK WAS PROFOUNDLY QUIET - BUT QUIETLY PROFOUND

6th year of conversation after Jack's transition

**ILLUMINATION**

**MY FAITH**
*generates a love in me*
*I would not*
*otherwise have.*

**DECEMBER 1, 2013 -8:20 A.M.**
My Jack was profoundly quiet – but quietly profound

## A MAN OF FEW,
## BUT POWERFULLY, MEANINGFUL WORDS
## – ON EARTH, AS IT IS IN HEAVEN

*I believe my Jack has something to say, that is worth listening to.*

*Jack: You are so kind to me, as you always were, but over here we see so much, and I wanted to share with you because I know 'IN YOUR WAY', you will inform the people.*

*"PEOPLE", LISTEN, FOR WE ARE 'ALL', ALWAYS HERE*

*– WITH YOU – DON'T MISS THAT LEVEL OF UNDERSTANDING*

*BECAUSE IT WOULD MEAN SO MUCH 'TO US'.*

*WE ALL TRY IN OUR OWN WAYS TO ACKNOWLEDGE*

*AND MAKE OURSELVES KNOWN, BUT 'MOST OF YOU'*

*SIMPLY DON'T BELIEVE THAT THIS IS POSSIBLE –*

*AND I WANT YOU TO KNOW THAT 'IT IS'.*

*AS ABOVE, SO BELOW, FOREVER MORE."*

*Jack*

§

## SAME DAY – 10:30 P.M.
**Smiles for me**

I am very kind to the raccoons no matter how much work they cause for me with their 'break-ins' and their babies who make so much mess and are so destructive in the Spring time. I always go out of *The House* at night to put an extra bowl of dog food and biscuits for them, no matter the weather. This evening, I have just done this and noticed something not witnessed before – but the snails seem to come out at night and whatever scraps are left on the plastic platters from the early morning feeding, the snails are devouring. I have to assume even snails can smell – wonders I continue to discover. Just a mention here because this is something I don't believe many of us know about.

§

## DECEMBER 3, 2013 – 5:06 A.M.
**Living in past happiness**

Dear God,
I know completely that YOU know what YOU are doing; I just wish I knew what I was doing. Some days and some nights, I am still so lost – so consumed with missing my perfect mate – I roam our house touching and kissing his pictures and remembering when and where they were taken, and the happiness felt at that time. I seem to live in past happiness because it was so great and so meaningful and so lasting and yes, I have happiness now, but by comparison – it is fleeting. My beloved Jack had such depth, such strength and on some days, I do too, but it is something I have grown into and it is not yet a lingering part of who I am. I am becoming like him, but still have a way to go. He is telling me that is not so, and that I already have what he seemingly had, but to my thinking – I have not consumed enough strength yet to maintain it.

*Jack: I disagree completely. You never, ever gave yourself the credit that you are due. Stop now and reconnect to the love vibration of yourself, as well as of God and me. Sweetheart, your memory is not serving you as it should. You forget, you disconnect, and are not practicing what you preach.*

§

## DECEMBER 4, 2013- 10:40 P.M.
### *Digit* is in Heaven

Me: Our beautiful *Digit* made her transition last night while in her building, *The Barracks*. It was good that she was in her building, on the carpet and that the night was warm. Travis (a son of our well serviceman) was here helping me and for the first time, he assisted with the burial in our precious *Memorial Park*, and talking about precious, my favorite little cat **Mittens** was with us at the cemetery also.

*Jack: He enjoyed being part of the group, truly his attitude has changed.*

Me: That's for sure because about a year ago, I thought his time on Earth was over. He was at that time so thin and unsociable, but his body has changed with the consumption of so much food and milk, and I am just plain thrilled with him. Travis was here to get corn (to save me time) because this weekend we may have an ice storm, and I don't want to go out in that kind of weather.

*Jack: Good choice My Sweet, and yes our precious baby is here and more alive than when she was with you.*

Me: You know of her last night on Earth, she was active and eating and so, she did live in her usual way until the end. I tried hundreds of times to pet her and most of the time she avoided the touch or struck out at me. I forgive her completely and hope I did enough to make her life happy.

*Jack: Don't go there – she was blessed and knew it.*

§

## DECEMBER 6, 2013
### I want to 'be me'

Me: I don't want to be what someone else wants me to be – I want to be what I want to be for myself.
*Jack: And so you should.*

§

## DECEMBER 10, 2013 – 7:55 A.M.
### I had no idea we would be doing this kind of work
*Neither of us had any idea we would be doing this work – writing books. I was reflecting with Jack on our work with our soon-to-be third book, and the positive direction it was taking for our life.*

Me: I had no idea we would be doing this kind of work – writing.
*Jack: Neither did I. It takes both of us, as it did with all other business endeavors. Neither of us can do it alone – both of us 'with God', that is.*
Me: I am what I am, and I do what I do – by the Grace of God. It is the Father within who does the work.
*Jack: Good girl, wonderful girl. You are so right.*

§

## DECEMBER 2013
### To the World I Say

LIFE, TO ME, IS A PERSONAL JOURNEY – FOR IT IS YOUR OWN SOUL YOU ARE POLISHING. IT IS YOUR CHOICES THAT YOU MAKE FOR ITS GROWTH. The only rules I know are not to harm others.

I don't have to do things like you, and you certainly don't have to do things like me; however, if something I do, something I believe or say affects you in a positive way and helps you – I have done well.

WE JUST HAVE TO HELP EACH OTHER, ENCOURAGE EACH OTHER and SUPPORT EACH OTHER. However, IT IS A 'PERSONAL' JOURNEY TO POLISH and

SAVE OUR OWN SOUL.
I should not judge you, and you should not judge me for we do not know where we are at in our growth.

§

## DECEMBER 15, 2013 – 5:29 A.M.
## My first moment of 'knowing'

*I was remembering, June 7, 1988 – that first moment of knowing through your voice, that breath of fullest realization, something powerful here!*

For the record (my personal record) to honor my dearest and most beloved husband and soulmate Jack Farley, who this lifetime gave his all to me – everything he had within and without. He stretched and reached for the best of himself; for I know I demanded that of him without saying a word. As a result, he recognized what we have – that highest and deepest love that two souls can bathe in, God's love, Everlasting; and through that love, we have purpose and power in our lives. For years, I had been thinking it was Jack's power, but now I know, fully know and understand, it is GOD'S power 'through Jack'.

Me: Yes Jack, I love God more, and I live every day in that 'moment of knowing', through you and your voice. God used you to reach me.
*Jack: Good girl, to remind you, my girl – I too am fulfilled.*
*REMEMBER NOW, HE IS USING YOU TO REACH OTHERS.*
Me: I now know God loves me even more than you do, wow! Imagine that, if you can!

§

## MONDAY, DECEMBER 16 2013
## My rewards

I have to document this fantastic sight. It is 4 P.M. and there are, within sight, at least 6 doe sitting, lying or standing at the back of our house under the trees. It is the first day for many days where the weather is not freezing. It is about 55 degrees, and these beauties have found a place or space on the hay or leaves to sit in the late afternoon sunshine, and they are peaceful. These sightings always take my breath away. There must be a few remaining dried acorns - they are foraging for, because they are eating. These sightings for me are my rewards.

§

## DECEMBER 23, 2013 – 9:25 P.M.
## Our *Mittens* is a priceless gift that just 'keeps on giving'

To think that over a year ago I was preparing a coffin for him because he looked so down and out and would not eat. His fur was terrible because he had a saliva problem and could not clean himself properly. Well, I have pursued pampering, tempted with so many foods, mashing and mixing with milk, and now he has an appetite resembling a small horse. He drinks and drinks cat milk, eats baby food by the jar and this afternoon, I put out a plate of chicken and cooked turkey bacon scraps – intended for the raccoons, and I think he ate it all. He made me laugh so hard. He will allow me to pet him just about all I want, but I am not allowed to pick him up. He loves me so much, I know it. He sits at the glass door for several hours at a time just looking for my presence. What a blessing Jack, and I am so glad I am attentive and recognize this growth. He knows of my love, and I know of his – just as I know of God's love, and he knows of ours.

§

## DECEMBER 26, 2013 – 8:09 A.M.
**I love being used!**

Many people compliment me on our writing achievements. They don't understand, and some won't understand it is not me at all – it is the Father within who does the work because I am willing to be used. I love being used – I am His instrument. JACK AND I ARE BOTH 'HIS' INSTRUMENTS TO GET THE WORD TO THE PEOPLE THAT THERE IS NO ENDING AT DEATH. JACK IS ABOVE, AND I AM BELOW, AND IT IS THE SAME – AS ABOVE SO BELOW. Everyone has this connection, this possibility, yes, everyone – it is a matter of allowing, tuning in and accepting what comes. It is truth, and it is wonderful to never feel alone even though we appear to be.

The only thing I want, while still on the Earth plane, is someone who thinks like me, who would enjoy my company – preferably a gentleman who knows God, with strength to help me with the animals and this magnificent land. Jack and God tell me he is there preparing himself for the task of me – no easy task, but willing to share what I am and what I know. He must be in the space of hard work with Earthly chores and believing for the spiritual.

§

## SUNDAY, DECEMBER 29, 2013 – 7:35 A.M.
**Beautiful sights, yet again**

It is cold, it is winter, yesterday it rained a lot and the bird seeds were washed away; however, some remained on one of the tables. As I was peering out between the venetian blinds, there was a beautiful, magnificent blue bird sitting in the middle of the remaining seed eating! Yes, to me, a beautiful sight this Sunday morning. There were hootie owls this morning telling me to "get up", and at least 9 deer standing across from our house, staring at the door – I assume looking for me. It cannot be said enough that I Love God's chosen work for me.

§

# CHAPTER 17
# 2014

# DO NOT BE ANXIOUS

7th year of conversation after Jack's transition

## ILLUMINATION

*Do not be anxious beforehand*
*about what you are to say,*
*but say whatever is given you in that hour*
*– for it is not you who speaks,*
*but it is the Holy Spirit*

*- Mark 13:11*

§

*God is the only way,*
*for God is all there is.*
*Everything is God.*
(Jack's words in my ear is all I know.)

§

## JANUARY 1, 2014
## To the World I Say

It is a new year in time and space, and I plan to make every day count. GOD'S GRACE is all there is for me. Life is at its best when I live it this way.

## LATER

Sleepless nights are not necessarily good nights, but last night was a good night for me, even though it was sleepless. I was in touch with God and Jack, learning so much about myself. I flew over mountains in my understanding. We are all 'monsters of our own making', and I am still rebuilding what I made 70 years ago, as a child and under my mother's control and 'her' fears.

If you are really searching for the truth, you will find it – if at times only temporary because the flesh still holds us, but I am finding you can loose <u>all</u> the ties that bind.

§

## FRIDAY, JANUARY 17, 2014 – 1:07 P.M.
## Thank you for revealing your presence to me

*Let it be known that as I came out from the office, the sun was shining brightly, and I saw on the ground the shadow of a butterfly circling my head. I stood still because I wanted to witness what I knew to be my husband's spirit and as I stood and looked at a large metal sign on which is printed (GOD AND ANIMALS RULE HERE…), I noticed that the butterfly settled on the word 'GOD'. It took my breath away but then made me smile because I knew GOD, JACK and I ARE ONE!*

§

## SATURDAY, JANUARY 18, 2014 – 11:55 A.M.
## I am truly blessed – Jack proved he has my back

*The very next day, Saturday, January 18 at exactly 11:55 A.M., I was once again exiting the office with my right hand full of mail. I had my right hand extended and my left hand ready to open the lock on the front gate and as I walked past the that sign indicating 'GOD AND ANIMALS RULE HERE…', I felt the rush of what I now know to be Jack's spirit circling my head, and this day he landed on the mail in my right hand as I was taking it to the mailbox. He circled two or three times before making his landing. I feel the breeze of his wings as he flies across my face. Again, I gasped, slowed down and allowed him to stay on the mail for as long as he wanted. He, then, went ahead of me, came back around my head and flew up into the trees – once again, a remarkable experience and confirms that he is 'always here'!*

§

## JANUARY 22, 2014
## Today I am healed and into 'my own power'

*(I want my Jack to fly higher – he can and does when I do 'this')*

**To the World I Say**

*Let it be known that this day I truly 'love me'.*

On this Earth plane, as I speak, I am the most interesting person I know! Of course, I have met others more interesting, from whom I have learned, and I know there are others I have not yet met, but as of this moment in time – I am the most interesting. (Laugh – but it's true).

My life experiences from my childhood to this day are fascinating – I fascinate myself when I recall them. I never know what thought is going to come next – and the memory recall with or without Jack that is going to linger and give me pause to reflect and learn from. 'With my Jack and where he is now', it is indescribable – what he tells me in secret, and in my writings. I am blessed beyond what is normal. I am in tune with the infinite.

My good comes to me under Divine Law and in right timing. I know and accept this.

I know that every discomfort I experience in my body is the result of my programmed thinking in my mind from childhood. I am now willing to release the patterns in my consciousness that created in my mind the conditions of present pain or discomfort. I am in charge; I can feel God's breath and most certainly Jack's. The LIGHT OF GOD surrounds me. The LOVE OF GOD enfolds me. No one can remove it (my pain), except me by my fearless thoughts. I no longer allow fear to invade my conscious awareness. I claim God's Power, and I claim it NOW. The almightiness of God through the Christ in me heals my mind and body right now – and so it is in Jesus name. The power that made my body heals my body – it happens no other way, this I know. I am joyful, loving being me – a woman, a small but powerful woman.

## LATER
### I plan to be my 'highest and best'

Everybody is or should be doing all they can to help others (never forgetting the precious creatures whose habitats we are invading). But how are we feeling about ourselves? Where is our vibration – where is yours? Are we in the highest and best space that we can be, are we fearless or fearful? When we are in the fearful space, love cannot exist. Remember perfect love casts out fear, so 'stay in the 'love vibration' for this is where you meet God. See what happens when you do this.

§

## JANUARY 24, 2014 – 8:32 A.M.
### For me, wonders will NEVER cease

In warm sunny Texas, we have been experiencing artic blasts with unusual winter storms of ice and thin coatings of snow. This morning I was peeking through the blinds and low and behold, on the tile patio just outside the front of our house, I saw a raven who had just discovered the cat food from the previous day that was obviously frozen cold, but still available to the eye of this magnificent bird. Yes, he had his daily bread that the evening raccoons either missed or didn't come out to eat because of the freezing rain. He had to <u>work</u> to get it – just like us.

§

**JANUARY 28, 2014**
**Questions about the unusual weather**
*I was thinking about the weather and how seriously bad it has been this winter all over the country and was wondering if God was upset with us.*

Me: God, are you angry with me?
**GOD: No My Child. You continue to learn. Disobedience brings others grief. There are laws and rules that are not obeyed. This is being taught.**

§

# CHAPTER 18
# 2014

# THE FLESH IS A HINDRANCE
## – TO OUR GROWTH

7th year of conversation after Jack's transition

## ILLUMINATION

*The orthodox mind
condemns anything it does not understand.*

*- Einstein*

## SUNDAY, JANUARY 25, 2014 – 10:54 P.M.
### I KNOW that I'm still growing

**To the World I Say**

*Sometimes*, especially late at night for a few brief moments when my entire being hungers for the warmth and the touch of my beloved husband – I don't care about my soul. All I want is my evolved, sensitive, adoring husband with his glistening love-filled eyes gazing at me, telling me in his sensuous, soft voice, that he loves me still. I miss his voice. All I want are his warm arms to surround me, yes, that's all I want – his attentiveness to my needs whatever they may be at that moment, however trivial. He could cast fears and doubt away with a word or a touch. For those few brief moments of wanting what was – his breath on me – that is all I need.

Most people want what they want, and they want it now and this just confirms for brief, very brief moments that I am still there, too – for it is the flesh that holds us in this space. The flesh is a hindrance to our growth, no doubt about it.

When I take that deep breath of faith and knowing, I realize without doubt, that I still have my Jack for he continues to talk to me, direct me, comfort me especially when he appears over my head in vibrant butterfly form, around me, in front of me, on my hand or on the mail I carry to the mailbox. He has my back! He still makes his presence known so frequently and always when I am enveloped in the stresses of everyday living and when I have for the moment, forgotten him. It is like he 'insists' on reminding me, "*Hey, I'm still here.*" I am so blessed to know the goodness of him.

For seven years now, since his transition, I have continued every second of every day to care about the creatures, domestic and wild. I extend myself in every way possible – even in the ice storms of late, to put their needs first. They reward me when they allow me to touch them, and when they reveal that they trust me.

I am no saint, and I do not pretend to be – I am God's instrument, and <u>He works through me</u>; however, I am still in the flesh with deep feelings of loss, no matter how it should be said. I miss my husband after seven years, and some days I still find him any way I can. <u>Let it be known that I know better, and let it be known that I know when I do this</u> – but <u>let it be known at times the power of the flesh holds strong and the will surrenders, if only for a short while</u>.

I am reminded daily that <u>I am still growing</u>.

§

## JANUARY 26, 2014
### Learning never ceases – for soul growth is never ending

<u>Jack assures me that there is so much more "*beyond life as we know it*," and the so-called death experience</u> – <u>as we understand it</u>, and that <u>the journey for each one of us continues</u>. <u>There is so much to learn, and learning never ceases in this world or the next</u>. There is no ending, denying, escaping – we are all caught in the web and will eventually – through many lifetimes – come into the space of light and freedom of knowing all there is. <u>Soul growth is never ending</u> – Jack is still learning that he could have been better, he could have done more. <u>I</u> saw him as perfect, but he now knows he could have been better, and he could have done more. Yes, my indescribably perfect Jack is not perfect at all. He is still learning for as he says so many times, "*Learning never ceases*."

To be in the space near God, is an endless journey of perfection for He is just that. As much as I love my Jack, I love God more. I declare I do, and this makes Jack happy.

*Jack: Indeed – my wife has no unspoken thoughts.*

§

206

# CHAPTER 19
# 2014

# HOW TO STAY IN THE LOVE
# VIBRATION
## - <u>MY</u> WAY

**7th year of conversation after Jack's transition**

## ILLUMINATION

*I want to know God's thoughts –*
*the rest are details.*

*- Einstein*

**MAKE YOUR MANTRA:**

**"HIGHEST   AND   DEEPEST"**
*(LOVE, that two souls can bathe in)*

Meditate on these two words alone –
you will rise above the pain and sorrow
of your personal life.

Be in the arms of <u>your</u> Savior
whoever that might be for you –
for it is a choice for each one of us.

You will sleep peacefully,
and wake up from the worlds you will have traveled to –
from that <u>perfect rest</u> – <u>of God's loving arms</u>.

You will continue to LIVE in <u>HIS POWER</u>,
and once again REST in <u>HIS LOVE</u>.

It is always your choice.

<u>GOD'S GRACE</u> will bring you success
if you give it the pipeline of <u>YOUR FAITH</u>.

<u>It is always 'your' choice.</u>

**MAY GOD BLESS YOUR CHOICES**

§

**HOW TO STAY IN THE LOVE VIBRATION (<u>my</u> way)**
How to reach this vibrational space of LOVE
where we can talk to and hear from 'the other side' –
<u>is very simple</u> –
automatic, once you calm down and breathe deeply.

It is not work, it is just the opposite;
it is letting go of the world's cares
and focusing on the heart center –
<u>receiving</u>, <u>understanding</u> and <u>giving love</u>.


**IT IS AN EXCHANGE**
❖　 a 'letting go' of the pressures of living
❖　 visualizing them float away
❖　 <u>allowing</u> yourself to <u>accept</u> the <u>goodness</u> and LOVE OF GOD
❖　 feeling buoyant and carefree

In this space, we can connect <u>with God, and our loved ones</u>.
This is the space of meditation – 'SELF-MASTERY'.
<u>Not a matter of doing</u>, <u>but BEING</u>.

§

A PRAYER:　　GOD:

Remove my fears.

Fulfill my needs.

Give me total belief

in <u>YOUR POWER WITHIN</u>

to make all things well.

And so it is.

§

PEOPLE:

BEHAVE

as if GOD'S presence in all life matters

– because it does.

§

Amen and Amen.

§

# CHAPTER 20
# 2014

# SOUL GROWTH AND PERFECTION
## – AS I SEE IT

### 7th year of conversation after Jack's transition

## ILLUMINATION

*The only permanent object you possess is <u>your soul</u>*
*— all else is impermanent.*

<u>**This is ALL you take to Heaven.**</u>

To the World I Say
<u>MY</u> definition of SOUL (through Jack),
<u>the highest and deepest part of you</u>

THE UNSEEN, INDEFINABLE YOU.
– THE ENERGY, THE LIGHT (OR DARK)
THAT RADIATES HOW YOU ARE.
HOW YOU HAVE GROWN IN THE CHRIST-
CONSCIOUSNESS
– THE SPIRITUAL PART OF YOU.
SPIRIT PART – IS THE ONLY PART THAT MATTERS.

CHRIST IS THE EXAMPLE OF HOW WE SHOULD BE
– OUR BEST!

WHAT OTHERS FEEL FROM US,
WHEN IN OUR PRESENCE,
ATTRACTED OR REPELLED.
TOO MUCH LIGHT CAN REPEL THOSE OF DARKNESS.
THEY DON'T UNDERSTAND LIGHT AS
THOSE OF LIGHT DO NOT UNDERSTAND DARKNESS.

§

## FEBRUARY 14, 2014 – 6:35 A.M.
## Valentine's Day

### To the World I Say

The Mission (at **CAT HAVEN**), 'our' Mission continues – and it is my fervent prayer that it will, forever – on this priceless small parcel of land.

The Message, 'our' Message changes as we grow; and for me, it becomes ever more clear as my understanding of life and its meaning becomes more clear. Not everyone thinks like me, and I accept that for everyone's journey is personal for the growth of their own soul. Now in my present physical form, I have more than a profound understanding of how I am growing 'my soul' – and I know that I am.

I AM more, Jack is more – and I believe on 'both sides' that Jack and I are still polishing 'our' souls!

Since Jack's transition from this Earth realm,
our understanding of each other has grown substantially.
His presence is felt in my every breath – yes, he is in me, as is God.
And yes, WE ARE ONE.

I FEEL IT, I BREATHE IT.

I KNOW IT IS EVERLASTING.

I am love; Jack is love, as is God, for we are created in His image.
I have confirmed in my learning that love is all there is, and it is
all we should be living for
– to love and be loved – I am there.

I know what it is like to be loved – and there is nothing like it.
I wish for all what I know and what I have. No amount of money
brings that forth.

> I have learned to love myself,
> I am consumed with love for my Jack
> but I have learned to love God more,
> for this is where true happiness reigns.

*Jack: From brilliance to illumination, my – what perfection I see! Your love is taking me higher. As I have said before, there are worlds beyond worlds out here – beyond what technology has yet revealed. Unknown until you are here, and it is a wonderful place and space in which to be. Tell the people to keep growing for the journey is not an easy one, but the vision is clear once you get here.*

*God has us, 'all of us' exactly where He wants us to be, here or there journeying and doing His Will never ceases – along with the learning.*

*We both knew eons ago that no amount of money gets you into Heaven. So many weak souls stay fooled by this. Their next life will bring them down to a reality they have no awareness of, right now. Unless they use the money to help the world, they will suffer consequences. It is God's money and not theirs. Some are aware of this and make tremendous strides for improvement of mankind. Others make no strides for improvements to others, but only for themselves. They will suffer – have no doubt. God knows what He is doing when He gives what man desires. He tests us when He gives and when He takes away – and He will. Those who seemingly 'have' have nothing unless they use it well. And those who seemingly have little but whose hearts are pure, have everything.*

Me: Thank you Sweetheart and thank you God that I know this and may I live accordingly.

My life is infused with magic
– and yours can be too for everything is exactly as it should be
for you to learn and grow
– JUST BELIEVE.

Jack tells me so often that absolutely everything is exactly as it should be,
everywhere, for everyone,
and if we don't like it,
it is presenting us with the opportunity to change it,
make it better, polish it and in so doing – polish ourselves
– the soul of us.
This is how we become more like Christ.

We must recognize the God in all life and all of life's events.
There is a message for us to learn, obey and improve.
God never punishes, but he does teach.

We must be willing to learn,
not what is written in text books
but in life's lessons
– whether they appear good, or not as good as we would prefer.
We must BE, and DO our best.

FOR THIS IS WHAT GOD EXPECTS
– AND THIS WE MUST DO!

§

# CHAPTER 21
# 2014

# MY VOWS TO JACK
### November 14, 1989

## NOVEMBER 14, 1989
## My vows to Jack

*Let it be known that Jack's wedding vows to me of this date, November 14, 1989 are displayed on the back cover of our first book,* Listen, I'm Still Here *– Part I and herein, our third book, includes my vows to Jack.*

### ACKNOWLEDGING GOD AS OUR WITNESS
### – IN THIS HOLY PLACE

I am love.  You are love.
We are ONE love.  Love is all there is.

For as long as we both are LOVE – above all others, Jack Farley,
I will continue to honor, respect, trust and cherish
- - but never possess you.

The LOVE that I am will always allow 'us' space in which to grow
in God's likeness.  This growth to be the foundation of our union.
What we have when we die we leave to others
– what we 'become' is ours, forever.

For 'all time' – my LOVE will 'allow' you to 'be'
who you are meant to be.
My LOVE 'accepts' that being.  True love allows.  True love accepts.
My LOVE for you is true.

I will not, with intention, ever try to change who you are,
only to understand more about myself, through you.
I ask only that we reason our differences with alternate solutions.

I attach no importance to your yesterdays,
but simply relish what you have become through them.

At no time will I over-emphasize the physical,
realizing that 'we are not a body'.
We are spirit beings, as God created us - -
perfect in every way through eternity.
Joyfully, I will care for you,
doing my best to place your needs above my own.
Being at all times your best friend,
and never your servant.

Jack Farley - -
I adore you.  I admire you.  I respect you.
I am thrilled and inspired by your  strengths,
creativity, sensitivity, generosity, and humor.
My heart is humble for all the gifts of yourself that you bring to me
and it overflows with joy and gratitude

for the genuinely 'happy' LOVE you show me,
and I know, the best is yet to come.

I will always make time for you - -
Your hopes, dreams, victories and losses,
and trust we will make time to encourage
the hopes and dreams of others,
and 'together' comfort them in their losses.

I gladly share with you, now, and always,
those things and gifts I possess,
but trust we will always include and consider others in our blessings.

You are a 'gift from God' to me. I see God in you.
Through you, I am able to see the 'God part of me'.

I treasure you, and give thanks to the Source.

I feel your LOVE for me, now.
I know you cherish me, as I cherish you.
I need your power - - you need my wings.

Jack Farley – I choose to be by your side in this lifetime
– your partner – your wife.
I choose to grow to God with you by my side.

As husband and wife (as was with the Fillmore's)
"may we dedicate ourselves, our time and our money
– all we have and expect to have,
to the spirit of truth.
It being understood
that the said spirit of truth
shall render unto us
an equivalent for this dedication,
in peace of mind, health of body, wisdom, understanding, love, life,
and an abundant supply of all things necessary to meet every want
without our making any of these things the object of our existence."

May we LOVE 'always' as ONE with the universe.

In this truthful, memorable and 'happy' moment in time, know,
I AM LOVE WITH YOU

With God's blessing and in God's Light
this is my LOVE filled dedication to you this day, November 14, 1989.

Dorothy Ann Rose

AMEN AND AMEN

# EPILOGUE

**2014**

**ILLUMINATION**

**DEATH – TRANSFORMATION**
*Do it with GRACE,*
*SERENITY*
*and EXCITEMENT*
*about where the new journey*
*is going to take you.*

*Not my words – but a total summation of my learning.*

# EPILOGUE

Me: GOD, I love this place and space we named CAT HAVEN – my Garden of Eden – that my Jack built with his creative talent and so much love. This space is one loving couple's creation to make the world a better place.

GOD, You gave us the land which we gave right back to you with our solemn promise to care for every creature who ventured onto it. It is so pure, so innocent, so lovely, so intended for the care of your creatures, great and small – who are forgotten by so many. All we both want is that it forever more be intended for the sacred purpose of loving care – never neglected or invaded by those whose hearts are not pure. Even outside our gates there is selfish neglect and no understanding of the beauty this small parcel of land contains.

GOD, bring only those who are in their right mind to continue our work and our intentions – people of understanding of the needs of the lowest hearts of understanding.

*Jack: Sweetheart, never fear, the right ones have already been selected for eons to come. We have done the ground work, we built the foundation and you most certainly can relax and know our work, God's work, will be continued <u>in our ways</u>. It is all planned and blessed.*

Me: I know what disappointment is; I know what betrayal is for I have been so let down by others I trusted. Right now, I am trusting the unknown and unseen!

*Jack: You are trusting my wisdom and that of God, both of which you now know of. Yes you do and our work, your work will not be in vain. It is a done deal. There are those special people who will do what we have done – trust me and trust God. The good works, our good works, will never die. And yes My Love, the right ones are coming.*

Me: Your most beautiful hands built this small, but priceless space, with gifts inherited from your grandfather. I love you and your works so much.

*Jack: Sweetheart, love of all my lives, I know – but remember, always <u>LOVE GOD MORE. YES, DO THIS FOR TOGETHER WHEN WE LOVE HIM MORE – THERE IS THE POWER FOREVER MORE. AND SO I SAY TO YOU, LOVE GOD MORE. TRUST MY LOVE, AND BELIEVE, FOR THIS IS TRUTH.</u>*

§

# MY POSTSCRIPT

**To the World I Say**

No one can know what I know
and no one can feel what I feel
unless they have lost from this Earth realm to the next dimension
– their love of all lives,
their truest soulmate,
highest and deepest love.

No one can have exposed themselves to this level of learning
without that 'seeming loss'
– when it should be recognized as 'no loss',
only of the meaningless flesh
which is a hindrance to all existence,

– but most have no idea of this.

# MY PRAYER

LORD, IN THE DAILY ROUND OF COMMON TASKS

THE LITTLE NIGGLING NEEDS THAT EACH DAY BRINGS

GIVE ME A SPIRIT THAT WILL RISE, I ASK

ABOVE THE TYRANNY OF THE 'LITTLE THINGS'

THOSE LITTLE THINGS – THE PETTY JARS AND FRETS,

TRIVIAL CARES THAT MAKE UP OUR DAY,

DISAPPOINTMENTS AND SMALL UPSETS

THAT PRICK THE NERVES

AND TONGUE AND TEMPER FRAY

GIVE ME THE VISION THAT I MIGHT SEE

BEAUTY, IN HOMELY TASKS

IN WORK THAT IS WELL DONE,

AND HELP ME TO ACCEPT MY LOT

AND NOT WISH FOR AN EASIER ONE

§

*Not my creation of words, but sent to me by my mother over 40 years ago. She had found this in a British women's magazine. I hereby give credit where credit is due, but I learned from them and thank whoever wrote them so many years ago.*